Comments on other *Amazing*

"*Tightly written volumes filled with lots of wit and humour about famous and infamous Canadians.*"
Eric Shackleton, *The Globe and Mail*

"*The heightened sense of drama and intrigue, combined with a good dose of human interest is what sets* Amazing Stories *apart.*"
Pamela Klaffke, *Calgary Herald*

"*This is popular history as it should be... For this price, buy two and give one to a friend.*"
Terry Cook, a reader from Ottawa, on **Rebel Women**

"*Glasner creates the moment of the explosion itself in graphic detail...she builds detail upon gruesome detail to create a convincingly authentic picture.*"
Peggy McKinnon, *The Sunday Herald*, on **The Halifax Explosion**

"*It was wonderful...I found I could not put it down. I was sorry when it was completed.*"
Dorothy F. from Manitoba on **Marie-Anne Lagimodière**

"*Stories are rich in description, and bristle with a clever, stylish realness.*"
Mark Weber, *Central Alberta Advisor*, on **Ghost Town Stories II**

"*A compelling read. Bertin...has selected only the most intriguing tales, which she narrates with a wealth of detail.*"
Joyce Glasner, *New Brunswick Reader*, on **Strange Events**

"*The resulting book is one readers will want to share with all the women in their lives.*"
Lynn Martel, *Rocky Mountain Outlook*, on **Women Explorers**

CHAMPIONS OF WOMEN'S RIGHTS

AMAZING STORIES®

CHAMPIONS OF WOMEN'S RIGHTS

Leading Canadian Women and Their Battles for Social Justice

Moushumi Chakrabarty

HISTORY

James Lorimer & Company Ltd., Publishers
Toronto

James Lorimer & Company Ltd., Publishers acknowledges the support of the Ontario Arts Council. We acknowledge the financial support of the Government of Canada through the Canada Book Fund for our publishing activities. We acknowledge the support of the Canada Council for the Arts, which last year invested $20.1 million in writing and publishing throughout Canada. We acknowledge the support of the Government of Ontario through the Ontario Media Development Corporation's Ontario Book Initiative.

Library and Archives Canada Cataloguing in Publication

Chakrabarty, Moushumi
Champions of women's rights : leading Canadian women and their
battles for social justice / Moushumi Chakrabarty.

(Amazing stories)
Includes bibliographical references and index.
Issued also in electronic format.
ISBN 978-1-55277-727-5

1. Women social reformers--Canada--Biography. 2. Women political
activists--Canada--Biography. 3. Women's rights--Canada--History--19th
century. 4. Women's rights--Canada--History--20th century. 5. Feminists--
Canada--Biography. I. Title. II. Series: Amazing stories (Toronto, Ont.)

HQ1455.A3C53 2011   305.42092'271   C2011-900774-6

James Lorimer & Company Ltd., Publishers
317 Adelaide Street West, Suite 1002
Toronto, ON, Canada
M5V 1P9
www.lorimer.ca

Printed in Canada

FSC
www.fsc.org
MIX
Paper from
responsible sources
FSC® C016245

Asit, always.

Contents

Preface

Women traditionally played the role of accompanist in the performance of Canadian life, but their story has all the elements of great drama. For a long time, the Canadian woman was relegated to a secondary position while the idea of Canada as a nation took shape from an amorphous gathering of immigrants and native peoples.

The period from the mid-1800s to the 1930s is exciting, though, because of the clear link that appears between the development of Canada as a nation, and the progress of women's struggles for emancipation. Before that, they were a subdued group who accompanied their male relatives across the oceans, setting up home in a land characterized by rugged beauty and severe weather. They bore the brunt of many a storm, both within and without the limited confines of their homes. They faced prejudices against their sex as men spoke louder and louder.

Thank heavens some women decided to rewrite the script! Feisty and strongly individualistic, they took it upon themselves to demolish boundaries, to march into courtrooms, medical schools and municipal offices, to knock on people's doors to convince them to join in their glorious but often wearisome struggle for equal rights. They were ordinary women—daughters, mothers and sisters, who had the courage to think for themselves and not to follow blindly in the steps of their male counterparts. The man could be their father or brother or husband, but he needn't be right all the time, they thought. They refused to allow the rest of the world to define them in terms of their male relatives.

Many of these brave women were motivated by a Christian viewpoint that pushed them into doing what they felt was their duty: to bring enlightenment. Others acted out of economic necessity. Some simply used their brains, having grown weary with lack of stimulation. Many women, too, used common sense when deciding to assert themselves and to demand their rights. They saw no earthly reason to not take up opportunities staring at them in the face, just because they were deemed to be "the weaker sex."

It seems preposterous to us now that women did not have the vote, or that they were not even considered "persons" under the law. How could they then contribute to society? Or were they too insignificant to have a voice in the public sphere? What was woman's role in the world, then? These and similar questions no doubt made many Canadian women lie sleepless after their day's work was done.

In the 1860s the country was just beginning to assume its own place in a world still dominated by mighty Britannia. Dominion status was imminent and, in many Canadians, there was the sense they were becoming a people, separate from, yet connected to the mother country. Immigrants were pouring into Canada from Europe and hardworking colonists were struggling to establish a semblance of control over the vast tracts of land with their harsh winters.

Historians recall how immigration, the advent of railways and a taxation system took root in the political and social landscape of the country. Huge prairie provinces and northern territories were made more accessible by the railways. Boomtowns like Winnipeg suddenly began to flourish, and some people got immensely rich by trading in textiles and speculating on the railways and land.

Though the rulers of the country, seated in Ottawa, tooted the horn of individualism, English was very much the flavour of the month. In all things there was a decided Britishness, very Victorian in outlook, with all the drama and the drudgery enveloping the august queen's name. Victorian manners dominated culture. What was deemed proper behaviour for women was strictly monitored by the establishment—which consisted, naturally, of men. Any woman who stepped outside the declared bounds was labelled and shunned. Patriarchy was deeply ingrained in the Canadian ethos.

Meanwhile, settlers farmed the land and established homestead-ranches upon the prairies, to grow towns and villages where, earlier, there had been habitation by Natives, long abandoned now for greener pastures, or unclaimed land prone to short summers and severe winters. They toiled in the stony soil of Grey County in Ontario, or put their labour into building barns for neighbours in Brandon, Manitoba. They grew corn, opened dry goods stores and attended quilting bees with their families. A sense of oneness grew, even though people lived far apart and there was so much backbreaking work on their own farms and homesteads.

Another event with far reaching implications happened around 1879. The plentiful buffalo, which had thrived on the prairies, disappeared, and the Natives moved on. The buffalo had been a source of food, clothing and shelter for the indigenous population. Many of them moved to the United States. As a result, large quantities of land became available and the government began encouraging settlers to move west and set up homes.

Why is it important that we cast a backward glance at the pioneers of the "women's movement," as it was later called? Throughout the world, the emergence of women as equal players on life's stage has helped in the advancement of a country. The more subjugated the women, the worse off the country. Socially and politically it seems imperative that women take their rightful place for a country to progress. The pioneers were the women in whose footsteps later generations of feminists followed. Simultaneously with the emergence of a national Canadian identity, women's voices became stronger in asking for their rightful share.

Preface

This book attempts to reconstruct the lives of the women who went against the flow, who refused to accept the strictures laid down by men, who laid the foundations of the sense of entitlement that, today, girls and women take for granted. These, then, were the first wave of feminists; and, though their movement had its shortcomings, they performed an essential service to Canadian women for all time. The life-stories of this first wave of feminists are important to us in the twenty-first century, because they provide us with glimpses into who we were, and how far we have come as a nation. The personalizing of history is a tool that helps us understand why certain social mores flourish or die away.

How different was the life of women and girls then, from ours? Many girls were home-schooled and spent their time doing chores on their parents' farm and minding their younger siblings. Those who came from privileged backgrounds had art lessons, and ponies to ride. The majority of hard-working parents could only provide the bare minimum and girls had to make their own soaps, do the laundry and cook their meals in freezing temperatures. Only those girls who were really keen on educating themselves would have spent their meagre leisure time with books. Most citizens at the time commonly subscribed to the view that there was a "White man's duty." So Christianity gained ground and religious affiliations became very important in social milieus. This was inculcated into the children, as well.

Then the cities began to beckon. With industrialization came a host of opportunities and problems. Life, as the early settlers knew it, began to morph into a different beast altogether. People flocked to cities where they tried to find work. Crime, disease and alcohol raised their ugly heads and set about shaking the foundations of Canadian society. The railways became important and suddenly the country opened up. Many women started to flood the cities in search of work. Immigrants from Europe poured into Halifax and Montreal. Factories sprang up, offering jobs to women and to men, but the conditions in these factories were execrable and women suffered a great deal because of poor working conditions and lesser pay than men.

Women's lot in life, whether in farms or cities, stagnated. There were few opportunities for betterment. On their family farms women might work throughout their entire lives, but they had no legal right over the property. The woman could be turned out at any time despite her years. As well, in the garment factories of Montreal women worked in deplorable conditions, facing sexual harassment or intimidation at the hands of male foremen. Most of them bore it quietly to keep their employment. Not all, though.

Canadian women saw where their duties lay and how the nature of their duties had changed with the times. Certainly, they were responsible for the rearing of their children and the smooth running of their homes and farms. But slowly they realized there was a world that went far beyond the boundaries of those farms. They needed a public voice, and many of them spoke out as they became aware of the importance of being seen and heard as a group.

They were convinced that the moral and physical upkeep of the family as a unit was in their hands. Collective action was the only way to narrow the gap that existed between the circumstances that prevailed and an ideal world where women could achieve their true potential. This "maternal feminism" has been denigrated by latter-day feminist scholars, but we should keep the movement's ideologies within the framework of their times in history. Like a Chinook wind waving through the wheat fields of Alberta, a new consciousness rippled through the minds of Canadian women, leaving few untouched.

The Great War exploded like a bomb in 1914. Canadian men went off to Europe to fight and women were left to run the farms and factories. More women found work apart from the usual teaching jobs. In cities and towns all over the country, women found work in record numbers. In offices, the advent of the typewriter meant a new efficiency in everyday operations and women began to be employed as typists and stenographers. Canadian women grew conscious of their capacities. They knew they could be just as capable and hard working as their menfolk.

The question of what constitutes "work" is one of great

contention. In fact, women's work, which traditionally consisted of caring for children and running the household, was
barely deemed legitimate in the patriarchal mode of thinking.
It had little value, it was felt, since it had no direct relation to
money. No woman got paid to look after her children or
the livestock on her family farm. Men's work was perceived
as being more important since the man brought home the
wages. With the advent of war, and the men away, women
began to take pride in their work and in their capabilities.

Some of the early feminists went a bit further, demanding a say in the running of their municipalities and villages.
They saw no reason to sit back and let the men rule them,
since it had become clear how well the women were managing their own affairs. Devaluation of women's work has often
been the norm, but these early feminists refused to accept
that. They actively agitated around the issues that caused
them the most grief.

One of the foundation stones of the early feminist movement in Canada was temperance. Through organizations
like the Women's Christian Temperance Union (W.C.T.U.),
women reached out in their communities to put a stop to
the evils of alcohol consumption by men. They were of the
opinion that alcohol had an immoral and immediate effect
on family lives, and that it was a social malaise to be curbed.
One by one, throughout the entire land, women joined the
local chapters of the W.C.T.U., staging protests against liquor

companies and urging men to give up alcohol. Organizing and running a movement like the W.C.T.U. gave them the confidence to concentrate on bigger issues like the vote.

The franchise is a right we take for granted today. But at that time women did not have the vote, and therefore had no say in affairs outside their homes. It was as if they did not exist in public life. Since women had no voice, government policies were often skewed away from female concerns. Women might have had certain ideas about how schools should be run, for instance, or how hospital funds should be directed, but, because women were more or less silent, their concerns and wishes remained suppressed. Women knew that to truly make a difference, their voices needed to reach outside of the home. So they asked for the vote.

Any discussion of the female franchise in Canada without referring to the Persons case is impossible. That was the seed from which grew Canadian feminism in all its manifestations.

Before 1929, women were considered non-persons. When early feminists wanted to be appointed to the Senate they were told that, according to the law, they were not "persons." British Common law, followed in Canada, stated expressly that women were "persons in the matter of pains and penalties, but not in the matter of rights and privileges." Naturally, this led to a great deal of agitation, resulting in the emergence of the Famous Five, as they came to be known.

These five Alberta women got together to challenge Canada's legal interpretation of the word "persons" in the *British North America Act.*

Emily Murphy, Nellie McClung, Irene Parlby, Louise McKinney and Henrietta Edwards formally protested against the customary interpretation of Section 24 of the *Act*, which stipulated that only "qualified persons" could be appointed to the Senate. Claiming historical precedent, the Canadian government had interpreted this to mean men only, denying women a chance to play their part in law-making. But the Famous Five were undaunted and took the case to the Supreme Court of Canada. Unfortunately, that court also declared that women, indeed, were legally "not persons."

But even this couldn't stop the five. They approached the Privy Council in England to review the case. In October 1929, to the great relief and joy of Canadian women, Lord Sankey ruled that women were indeed persons and could be appointed to the Senate. This gave impetus to Canadian women, who went on to claim their place in society in the forthcoming years.

As twenty-first century Canadians, we need to remember whose hands were those that shaped our society.

Chapter 1
Emily Stowe

"How do you plead?"

"Not guilty, my lord," declared Dr. Emily Stowe, in tones ringing with conviction. Her voice did not falter, her gaze was direct and of all the people crowding the courtroom that warm September morning in 1879, she was perhaps the calmest. Certainly big issues were at stake, a reputation was to be made or marred. The charges were serious, as were the emotions running amok in the Toronto courtroom where a band of women from the Toronto Women's Literary Club grew agitated. Judge Kenneth Mackenzie was forced to ask for order. Reporters sweated as they scribbled in their notebooks; the counsel for defence, D'Alton McCarthy and Nelson Gordon Bigelow, conferred furiously.

Dr. Stowe's daughter, Dr. Augusta Stowe-Gullen, sat impassive in the courtroom, betraying her nervousness only by a trembling of lips and a tightening of hands. Some of the men in the room muttered threats and curses to females in general but their deepest scorn was reserved for those females who worked as doctors or "healers."

The case in question involved a nineteen-year-old unmarried and pregnant Sarah Ann Lovell, a maid employed in Toronto, who consulted Dr. Stowe in May that year. She was found dead on an August morning in her mother's Deer Park home. The previous day she had returned from a shopping expedition to Eaton's on Yonge Street and had seemed in good spirits, the coroner recalled. The cause of death caused some bafflement among the attending physicians.

At the post mortem, it was discovered that Sarah was five months pregnant. Earlier, suspecting the illegitimate pregnancy, Sarah Ann's employer, a Mrs. John Avis, had discharged her after advising her to see a doctor. The doctor Sarah Ann Lovell saw was Dr. Emily Stowe, who prescribed medicines that she was taking regularly. There were no universal abortion laws in Canada at the time. Thus, in such a situation Dr. Stowe would have had only a few options open to her. She could have refused to see the patient and have her sent away, or she could have handed her over to the authorities. Instead, feeling sorry for the obviously distraught young girl, Dr. Stowe had prescribed a dose of hellebore, cantharides and myrrh. However, she stressed to the coroner, the dosage she prescribed was mild and would have had absolutely no dangerous side effects.

In her testimony, Dr. Stowe said, "[Sarah Ann Lovell] detained me for some time and ultimately I gave her a prescription to get her out of my house...I state positively that there was nothing in the bottle which could have harmed the girl. I gave her the prescription to prevent her going to another doctor with the object which had induced her to come to me, and also to quiet her mind...There was nothing in the prescription which could have produced any serious consequences to affect her condition in any way."

The very fact that Dr. Stowe was a female practicing medicine was brought up and debated hotly in court. Questions were asked whether Dr. Stowe's practicing was legal or not. She pointed out that she had been practicing medicine in Toronto for the past eighteen years. In the end, the judge ordered the jury to acquit Dr. Stowe. "The prisoner is entitled to the benefit of any doubt," noted Judge Mackenzie, and, while there had been a prescribing of drugs "there was no administering or causing to be taken," which is what Dr. Stowe had been charged with doing.

When the verdict was announced, Dr. Stowe's family and friends were jubilant. However, Dr. Stowe was not satisfied with the way things were in the Canadian medical field. For years she had been fighting the establishment, trying to make a dent in the institutions that taught the medical sciences in Canada. She herself had tried to get admitted to the University of Toronto's medical school, but was repeatedly refused on account of her being female. She ultimately went to study medicine at the New York Medical College and Hospital for Women.

Emily Stowe

Just a few months after the trial, in 1880, she was finally granted a licence to practice medicine in Canada. All those years of banging her head against the patriarchal medical establishment in the country had finally paid off. Her own daughter, Augusta, was admitted to the Faculty of Medicine at Victoria College in Toronto, eventually becoming the first woman to graduate from a Canadian medical school.

Growing up in a Quaker family instilled certain qualities in Emily Stowe, right from the beginning. She learned the value of persistence and hard work from her parents, Hannah and Solomon Jennings. They were practicing

Methodists but were originally Quakers, who had settled in Norwich, Ontario. The belief that women were as important as men in the scheme of things was instilled into young Emily and her siblings. All of them were encouraged to seek an education, and achievement in all areas was encouraged by the enlightened Jennings family. Emily worked hard with her siblings in the pioneer community of Norwich. Life included community awareness and helping neighbours settle into a new homestead.

In 1846, Emily started teaching in a rural school in Summerville, near Norwich, taking up the many duties that came with becoming a teacher. Her duties included keeping the children warm during the winter months, cleaning the classroom after school was done and reviewing students at different grade levels.

Emily wanted to educate herself more. Her wish was to go to university and to become a doctor. She had always been a good student and was sure that the University of Toronto would not refuse her entry simply because she was a female. She reckoned wrong, however. Though her application was turned down, she did not give up hope. She continued teaching with the aim of saving enough money to go to the Provincial Normal School for Upper Canada in Toronto. This would have the advantage of giving her a better standing when she reapplied to university, she thought.

After she graduated from the Normal School, much to

her surprise, Emily was offered the position of principal at a Brantford public school. She had the distinction of becoming the first woman principal of such a school in Canada. In 1856, Emily married John Stowe, a carriage maker by trade. She had three children, Augusta, Frank and John. But her home life was disturbed when her husband was diagnosed with tuberculosis, and the doctors prescribed that John Stowe be admitted to a sanatorium. It then fell to Emily to assume the role of main breadwinner in the family. This, she decided, was her best opportunity to go into medicine.

Women doctors were greatly needed in society, Emily knew. Many women did not visit a male doctor because of modesty or shyness. They would rather hide their symptoms or suffer in silence than visit a male doctor. Since the University of Toronto would not admit her as a student, she would have to leave for New York. That meant spending more money on her education. In the time that followed, Emily worked hard at her teaching job to arrange for enough money. The family had to deal with many hardships as Emily saved for the New York medical school. Her sister Cordelia helped out by taking care of the children while Emily was studying and working.

The New York Medical College and Hospital for Women proved to be learning grounds for Emily in more ways than one. Not only was she training in medicine, she also was realizing how the suffrage movement in America was linked with the goal of women having access to medical education. Medicine was so male-dominated that women were denied access to the profession, resulting in inequity. The suffrage movement in America was gaining strength with Susan B. Anthony and Elizabeth Cady Stanton pressing for women's right to vote, and Emily was inspired to bring the same fervor to the women's movement in Canada. Her husband, John, seemed to be doing better physically, so she threw herself into the suffrage movement whole-heartedly. At a meeting called by the American Society for the Advancement of Women in Cleveland, Ohio, she realized that this could be a call for her to start such an endeavour in her own city.

At the time, women's legal rights in Canada left much to be desired. Even a woman's rights within her own family were sketchy. She had a right to be supported by her husband if she was married, but had no say in the bringing up of children, the religion they chose or whether they were sent out to work. The husband could hand over the guardianship of the children to another party in his absence, even if his wife was capable of looking after them. All these laws struck Emily as extremely unfair. She had seen the work suffragists in New York were doing to raise awareness about issues like this and she resolved that Canadian women deserved no less.

Emily Stowe became a doctor in 1867 and returned to Toronto to practise medicine. She was however, not granted a licence. It seems strange to us that she could practise for so many years without a licence. However, historians guess that Dr. Stowe simply kept paying the required fine. Many women flocked to her practice and she was flooded with patients. She advertised the fact that she was a doctor specializing in the diseases of women and children. She became so successful that she had to move to bigger chambers, at 135 Church Street. The city's residents got used to seeing Dr. Stowe cycle through the streets with her black bag and umbrella, making house calls. Despite her very busy practice, Emily made time to give talks about women's rights all over southern Ontario. When women came to consult her about physical diseases, she took the opportunity to make her views about women's rights be known to them. Emily believed that boys and girls should have the same education.

In 1870, after repeated applications to the university, she and another woman, Jennie Trout, were finally allowed to attend classes. However, the two ladies barely had time to relax and enjoy their victory. They were harassed in the classes by the male students. Grotesque drawings, obscene remarks and horrible objects were used to embarrass and humiliate the women who had the temerity to attend medical school. Surprisingly, it was not only the students who kept at this campaign designed to daunt the strong-willed women—one of the professors also stoked the fires by telling distasteful anecdotes in class. He even subtly encouraged the male students' bad behaviour. It was difficult for the two women to face this hostile environment every day.

According to Emily Stowe's biographer, the students and the professor did not realize what they were up against. Emily had sacrificed a great deal to reach where she was and was not about to allow that to be spoiled by a bunch of misogynists. She decided she would not bear it any longer and, one day, told the professor in no uncertain terms that if this behaviour did not stop, she would be meeting with his wife to apprise her of the situation. The harassment stopped immediately! Emily's goal in attending courses at the University of Toronto was to get her Ontario medical licence. She succeeded in 1880.

Meanwhile, Emily's suffrage activities continued in full swing. In 1876, she established the first Canadian women's organization mandated to demand equal rights for women. It was named, curiously enough, the Toronto Women's Literary Club. The group, however, discussed matters other than literature. They chose to call themselves a literary club because they felt society was still unable to accept radical notions of women's rights. By calling themselves a literary club, they could carry on their activities and meetings undisturbed by the more orthodox elements in the city. They debated on suffrage, politics, health and economic independence for women.

By 1881, the club sent a delegation to the Ontario legislature to ask for women's right to vote. By the next year, they had persuaded the government to grant voting rights to unmarried women who had the requisite property qualification. Though this was not fully what Emily and her colleagues at the club wanted, they celebrated it as a small victory. Then Emily decided to push for a cause close to her heart—the opening of doors for women in institutions offering higher education. A petition to this effect was sent to the legislature in 1882 and, two years later, Emily and her club tasted success. Women began to be admitted to the University of Toronto by 1886-87.

Emily was still unsatisfied, because women were not being admitted to Canadian medical schools. She campaigned vigorously, presented petitions and raised awareness about this topic. The Literary Club threw off its cloak in 1883 and adopted a new name indicative of its true character—Toronto Women's Suffrage Association. Whenever she could, she went from house to house collecting signatures for this cause. Although, in truth, her daughter Augusta was a student at Victoria College Medical School, this could be attributed to Emily's influence rather than a systemic change. It was not yet the norm for women to qualify as doctors. The Association adopted a resolution that year: "…that medical education for women is a recognized necessity, and consequently facilities for such instruction should be provided."

On October 1, 1883, the Women's Medical College was inaugurated by Toronto Mayor A. R. Boswell at 289 Sumach Street. By 1895, this institute merged with its sister institute in Kingston and the Ontario Medical College for Women was formed with the purpose of training women to be doctors. It took until 1906 for the University of Toronto to finally accept women medical students.

The suffrage movement had started to lag as women became discouraged by the responses from the establishment. Whenever women petitioned for rights, they were turned down. Emily realized it was time to inject some new life into the movement. She invited Dr. Anna Howard Shaw, a famous American suffragist, to speak in Toronto, and the speech provided just the kind of boost that Emily had hoped for. Shortly after, the Dominion Women's Enfranchisement Association was formed, and Emily was elected president.

She struggled to find a sympathetic voice in the legislature. John Waters, a member of the legislature who tabled many bills for women's rights, proved to be an ally. Though they were not successful, at least it was a beginning. By 1890, all the women's groups in Canada met at the first Dominion Conference where issues central to the movement were showcased.

Emily retired from medicine in 1893 and devoted herself completely to women's suffrage activities. She continued to serve as president of the Dominion Women's Enfranchisement Association. Emily passed away on April 30, 1903, in her daughter's Toronto home. A fighter to the end, she had once written, "My career has been one of much struggle, characterized by the usual persecution which attends everyone who pioneers a new movement or steps out of the line with established custom."

Chapter 2
Amelia Yeomans

When Dr. Amelia Yeomans walked into the cell, which was painted a depressing yellow, she could barely make out the moaning figure on the single cot. Covered with a filthy blanket, the prisoner was only a skeleton of a man, with a straggly beard and rheumy eyes, a racking cough and a weakness in his demeanour. The warden grunted in annoyance as he informed the prisoner that Dr. Yeomans had come to visit him, as requested. With a clang, the door was barred, enclosing the doctor and the prisoner in that foul-smelling atmosphere. Dr. Yeomans sat on a chair, beside herself with compassion for this wreck of a man as he awaited death for some crime too terrible to be contemplated. Her eyes were troubled as the prisoner took a deep breath and tried to talk. Instead, a fit of coughing doubled him up and Dr. Yeomans hastily picked up the glass of water at the bedside. The water did not look too appetizing and she wondered whether the germs lurking in there would do more harm than the water would do good to the sick man. There was a plate of stale, hard bread. No sunlight ever entered the tiny cell, she thought. She knew the man was a criminal, but surely a semblance of decency could be provided to prisoners in Manitoba?

The prisoner had himself requested the administration send for Dr. Yeomans. He did not want a priest. Perhaps he believed in the genuine selfless service that the doctor provided for Winnipeg's poorest and wanted to experience that benediction in his last hours.

This was not a new situation for Dr. Amelia Yeomans. She was accustomed to getting calls from the city's down-trodden, visiting the lower end of the social scale in severely Victorian Winnipeg, administering succour, both physical and mental, to the citizens. The people in the city's infamous North End were used to seeing her at all hours with her hair neatly tied back, alighting from a buggy with her black bag containing her medicines and apparatus. It wasn't only Amelia who drove all over the city, attending to the women and children. Her daughter, Lilian, a qualified doctor, often did the same. They specialized in diseases of women and children, and midwifery. Together, the mother-daughter team had established a following among the city's poorer sections.

Dr. Amelia Yeomans was born in Montreal in 1842, the year Charles Dickens visited the city. Times in Montreal were not particularly conducive to peace then, specially with Anglo-French tensions simmering underneath. A garrison of twelve thousand British soldiers lodged in the city, and tensions persisted over the hangings of some French civilians by the British in Ste Eustache in 1837. The incendiary mix also included Canadian-American tension, prompting the governor at the time, Sir Richard Jackson, to increase the number of troops in his garrison. New immigrants from England and Ireland were pouring into the city regularly at the wharfs. With their boxes and luggage, they crowded around, leafing through the freely-available, government-issued *Emigrants Handbook for Arrivals at Quebec*, which gave general directions about how to proceed to Upper and Lower Canada. The handbook also warned all the new immigrants against unscrupulous agents posing as experts, who would fleece them of their possessions.

The LeSueur household, however, was ordered and comfortable. Amelia's father was Peter LeSueur, who worked as secretary at the Civil Service Commission, and her mother was Barbara Dawson. Amelia thus had an upper middle class childhood and lived in comfortable circumstances with her family, which included an older brother, William Dawson LeSueur. Later in life, he was to become a much-lauded civil servant, a fellow of the Royal Society of Canada and an essayist. In her home, the children's English and Huguenot parentage ensured that education and achievements were much lauded. Amelia was home-schooled, while her brother was educated in Latin and Greek at the High School of Montreal. She grew up with the usual accomplishments of young ladies of the time.

When she was eighteen, in 1860, Amelia met and married Dr. Augustus A. Yeomans of Ontario. He became an assistant surgeon with the rank of captain in the United States Army at the time of the Civil War (1861–1865). A daughter, Lilian, was born to the young couple. In 1862, they moved to the States. With the Civil War raging, Dr. Augustus Yeomans worked in horrendous circumstances. Along with other surgeons, he had to work long hours in the midst of much pain and suffering. Often the men who died had to be dragged out from the hospital tents and piled up on the street to be carted away, fifty or sixty at a time, to cemeteries where they were buried without any ceremony. Amelia, no doubt, heard horrific tales of suffering from her husband about this time.

Amelia became mother to another daughter, Charlotte, but in 1878 life took an unexpected turn when her husband suddenly passed away. Amelia was left a widow with two grown daughters, Lilian and Charlotte. Lilian had decided to study medicine like her father and, with no medical schools in Canada accepting female students at the time, she enrolled at the University of Michigan at Ann Arbor. But her tenure there wasn't a lonely one, because Amelia decided to join her daughter at the university. The mother-daughter team of medical students would have raised a few eyebrows.

During that time, the University of Michigan Medical School was the only one in the United States to operate its own hospital. It had the distinction of being one of the few medical schools in the country which admitted women, and followed a science-based approach. The school had opened in 1850, charging $5 a year for a two-year education in medicine. It was mandatory for medical students to know enough Greek and Latin to be useful in reading and writing prescriptions. Amelia's early studies in these classical languages proved helpful to her now.

Life at medical school wasn't easy for women, since notions of modesty and appropriateness were always involved. It was considered unseemly for women to be in proximity of men when discussions of human anatomy and natural functions were concerned. They often had to deal with hostile or obscene comments made by male students who considered women to be interlopers in an exclusively male domain. Of course, since they had each other for support,

Amelia and Lilian could simply ignore the bad apples among the students; but there are documented instances of women dressing and acting as men to get through their education.

Amelia and her daughter decided to settle in Winnipeg, Manitoba, after they finished medical school. Amelia graduated in 1883, while her daughter finished a year earlier. Amelia did not get her licence till 1885, but that year she cleared the examinations of the medical board in Canada and was named a member of the College of Physicians and Surgeons of Manitoba on February 23. Finally, she had her MD and she was licenced to practise.

Both the Yeomans decided that women and children would be a priority in their careers, so they specialized in midwifery and diseases pertaining to women and children. It was natural enough, since they lived in Winnipeg and witnessed the city's unbridled growth during the 1880s. With the growth came poverty, crime, prostitution and chronic unemployment. The poverty was grinding among some sections of the population. Sewage was nonexistent, medical facilities were inadequate and housing was often rudimentary. All this bred hopelessness and misery, which in turn resulted in crime and degradation. The growth of the city, the province's designated capital, was so rapid it was difficult for the administration to get a handle on the social problems. Many women were mothers, struggling to get by with low wages, a drunken husband and a brood of children. Prostitution was a way out for them. New immigrants who came with stars in their eyes about a rosy life in Canada were often dismayed when reality hit.

After the Canadian Pacific Railway steamed into the city in 1880, there was an explosion of growth. While it was true that people got jobs, it was equally true that it brought in its wake dirt and noise as the environment morphed from rural to urban. Industrial development and migration ensured that many tongues were spoken. Factories spewed polluted smoke into the air over the city. Some men were skilled labourers looking for work; some women took in lodgers to make ends meet. A lot of men made fortunes in real estate, textiles and railways. Conversely, many people were pushed further down the scale and imbalances grew greater. Public health problems in the slums spiralled out of control and, since there were many young women working and living alone in the city, reform-minded people became concerned about their morality. Social gospel predominated in the mindset of the city's Protestants. Many organizations sprang up in response to the times. For instance, the All People's Mission in the city's North End worked to win over new immigrants to Protestantism. Witnessing the problems engulfing Winnipeg first hand, they started offering fresh air camps, gymnasiums and classes for learning English.

Into this atmosphere, Amelia and her daughter practised a form of social medicine, where they studied the roots of the issues. They not only treated the physical manifestations, but also took into account the social situation. Venereal disease was a huge problem and Amelia battled on many fronts trying to stem that tide. In 1894, she helped in the founding of the Winnipeg Humane Society, which at the time worked for neglected children.

Like most reform-minded people, she viewed alcohol and its consumption with suspicion. She was convinced that alcohol was the root cause of much of the distress affecting families, and it was only natural that she would gravitate towards the temperance movement that was then sweeping the country. She joined the Women's Christian Temperance Union in the city and became a fervent supporter. Later, she became its president. She attended and led rallies, urging women and men to realize fully the dangers of alcohol to society. Along with her work with the W.C.T.U., she focused on the issue of prostitution. She worked towards closing down the brothels that flourished on McFarlane and Annabella streets, and was a vocal opponent, unafraid to bring the matter up in polite society. The Victorians of Winnipeg were deeply divided over her activities. Most were too embarrassed to be discussing such topics openly, in the parlours of upper-class homes. They could hardly comprehend how Amelia could bear to speak so plainly.

The Reform movement was in full swing in Winnipeg, in response to the quality of life in the city. Amelia was a

dedicated worker in this movement, pressuring the administration to levy fines on drunkenness and prostitution.

Advertising a lecture in Winnipeg's Selkirk Hall, Amelia
announced that it would be only for men. Naturally, the
announcement raised many eyebrows. Her reason was simple: she was going to speak of things quite un-Victorian and
rightly estimated that few women would have the stomach
to sit through her talk. She spoke of her recent visit to one of
the city's hospitals and how she had witnessed the sad state
of young women who had been "ruined" by the depraved
men of Winnipeg. It is possible that she described in some
detail the effects of venereal disease, a topic guaranteed to
turn most delicately nurtured women green. She then wisely
appealed to the men present to be chivalrous and to protect
those women who were being led astray. Her clever approach
ensured that many of the audience, inspired by her words,
praised her efforts and became determined to help out. But
when she wrote on the same subject in a W.C.T.U. leaflet, she
was attacked by women who believed she was quite over-
stepping the bounds of decency.

Amelia also came into contact with the large Icelandic
community that had immigrated to Canada in the 1880s.
These North Europeans had come to Canada in search of
a better life, since their population in their native country
was expanding rapidly and resources were dwindling. They
had settled in the west when the Canadian government had

agreed to offer them land and free transportation from eastern Canada. The Icelandic women were accustomed to voting in their country and, when they came to settle in Canada, had found themselves forced to give up that right. This bothered a lot of them and they readily joined hands with Amelia in her fight for female suffrage. She had realized how important enfranchisement of women was. Only when women had the vote could they hope to better their circumstances. Working with these women, she realized that the lack of voting privilege was only one of the problems they faced. Since they did not speak English, they had many other issues. Amelia was one of the first to realize the problems faced by non-English-speaking immigrants.

She had a tough fight on her hands when she fought for women's suffrage. Most men of the day had very set ideas about the woman's role in society. They thought that if she stepped out of the domain of the house chaos would prevail in society and the family as a unit would disintegrate. Many women were apathetic and would never consider joining hands with suffragists.

Amelia stated, clearly, that "women were the most adamant protectors of community morals, purity and righteousness and would use their votes accordingly. Participation in the political process would enhance their authoritative influence over their children and inspire greater respect in husbands, sons and daughters." To this end, she set up a provincial suffrage association. She was elected first president of the Manitoba Equal Franchise Association.

In her fight to win the vote for women, Amelia declared, "...suffrage has been and is the hardest of all reforms because it demands unselfishness in all men who support it." She took part in a mock parliament at the Bijou Theatre in Winnipeg, an event organized by the W.C.T.U.

By 1905, Amelia was living with her two daughters in Calgary, where Charlotte was a nurse. Neither Amelia nor Lilian actively practised medicine during their Calgary years, but Amelia remained active in causes relating to suffrage and temperance. She died at the age of 73.

Chapter 3
Henrietta Muir Edwards

Henrietta Muir Edwards stared at the flat prairie grainland of Indian Head, Saskatchewan, from the door flap of her tent. The endless blue sky seemed to meet with the brown land in the distance, buzzards hovered overhead and a clean fresh wind billowed the folds of her dress. It was 1883, and white Europeans had settled in this southeastern corner of the province only a short while ago. A few months later, the Canadian Pacific Railway would roll through this mid-sized prairie town and change its character forever.

It was not in her nature to be overly sentimental, but Henrietta could not help sighing as she cast a backward glance at her life before Indian Head. She had lived in bustling Montreal, first with her parents and then with her husband and children. She had been born in 1849 into an affluent family in that city. Like many fortunate young girls of those times, Henrietta spent her days reading, sewing, painting and attending church. Her background enabled her to cultivate her love for painting, especially on china. In fact, her flower paintings and miniature portraits of such illustrious Canadians as Wilfrid Laurier and Lord Strathcona had earned her many admirers. Her family sent her to study art in New York and she had an exhibition of her paintings in the Royal Canadian Academy.

Life would have continued in the same comfortable way for Henrietta but she also had a strong moral sense. She chose to become involved with organizations that helped women. Henrietta started questioning the established customs of the day that relegated women to the back seat. Around this time, many less fortunate men and women were flooding the city, looking for employment in the factories that were springing up like mushrooms. It was a move away from rural roots that led to displacement of people and to changing social mores. By the middle of the nineteenth century, women and children made up forty-two per cent of the industrial workforce in Montreal. Girls barely entering their teens were often sent to work in the city's many textile mills.

Henrietta grew aware of the massive disparity between

the lives of these women and her own. Long hours, poor pay and unsafe working conditions were the lot for these women. Most of the city's poor depended on factory work for their survival. There were no laws to protect their interests and the onus was on the women to protect themselves. Yet, after a day of work, then trudging off home to attend to the family's needs, many of them just existed from day to day. Many of the women who came to work from rural areas had a hard time finding their bearings in a city like Montreal. They had no way of entertaining themselves or of making friends. Many took to undesirable ways after falling prey to unscrupulous people who exploited their innocence. Henrietta was an evangelical Christian and was moved by the plight of these women. She believed in practising what she preached and started working with these women. Her passion for social justice grew stronger and she refused to succumb to the easy life of a socialite.

She decided that one of the most important things the women needed was a place where they could stay safe from harassment and intimidation by males. She convinced her father to buy a big house in downtown Montreal, which she converted into a haven for working women. Along with her sister Amelia, she founded the Working Girls' Association in Montreal, serving as its president for many years. The sixty-room hostel provided vocational, legal, employment and educational support to working ladies. This initiative fulfilled a need that young women had, to meet with other women and colleagues in a safe place after work. Reading rooms and boarding houses catering to women workers were also on her agenda.

She also launched a magazine for working women in the city. *Working Woman of Canada*, edited and published by her, was partly funded by the sale of her artwork.

In a speech to the Association she declared proudly, " Our Association Rooms (on) 73 Bleury Street have fully answered all our expectations in engaging them in so central a part of the city in the number of young women who take advantage of them, not only in applying for work of all kinds, but as a place of social intercourse. Some idea of their usefulness may be obtained when we state that the average attendance at them is over 1000 a month. The only paid worker is the Superintendent who can be seen from nine to six every day. All the members of the Association are young women who are supporting themselves by their own exertions."

In 1876, she married Dr. Oliver Cromwell Edwards and had three children, settling down to a life characterized by reform work, bringing up her children while keeping busy with her various hobbies like chess, taxidermy and amateur photography. She also had a deep interest in the study of Esperanto, an artificial language whose aim was to create universal harmony through a language common to all humanity. Her idealistic temperament had become apparent.

However, this pattern of life in Montreal was not to last long for the Edwards family. Henrietta's husband was appointed the first general medical practitioner for the Northwest Territories' Indian reservations. They were to move to Indian Head, Saskatchewan, with their young children. Her luxurious home, personal maid and all the creature comforts that she was accustomed to soon became things of the past. Henrietta found she had little spare time, what with caring for her children, William, Alice and Margaret, as well as keeping house in a tent near the aboriginal encampment.

The Natives, who lived in Indian Head before the Scottish settlers, had been cultivating corn for many years. Once the European fur traders and then the railway arrived, much changed in the town. Settlements were established and the Hudson's Bay Company brought out doctors to live and to serve in the nascent communities.

The doctors were paid fixed wages and granted lodging and subsistence for the first two years. They might be offered land if they were willing to settle there after that initial period. Life was not easy, either for them or for their families. They often had to travel across the flat lands in toboggans or sleds in winter while making their rounds. In summer, they used the horse and buggy as an ambulance.

Yet Henrietta found much to interest her during those years. She had a deep-rooted horror for luxurious living and apathy. Like many women of that period, she was convinced

Henrietta Muir Edwards

of her moral duty—she believed that, because she was fortunate, she needed to give back to the community. Joining the W.C.T.U. in 1886, she made temperance a key issue in her list of causes.

The Edwards moved again and in 1890 they were deputed to go to Ottawa. The nation's capital was a magnet for both the well-heeled and those aspiring to be noticed.

Life was sophisticated and charming for those who had money. Picnics and excursions beside the Ottawa River were frequent as men and women in elaborate Victorian dress spent a lot of time and money on social engagements.

Yet for the working class life was lived in ill-ventilated shacks that sweltered in the summers and froze in the winters. The streets were dismal in the severe winters, and as people shuffled off to their jobs at the lumber mills, diseases and crime were commonplace. The population of Ottawa was about forty-thousand in the 1890s and the backwoods town had not yet acquired the sophistication and grace it would later develop.

Henrietta did not blindly jump into the round of social events in Ottawa. Instead, she spent a lot of time studying Canada's laws. Her interests included prison reform, equal grounds for divorce and allowances for women. It was said that she knew more about laws affecting women in Canada than even the Chief Justice of Canada!

She met another amazing woman at the time, a new-comer to Canada, Lady Ishbel Marjoribanks Gordon. Lady Aberdeen was the wife of the Governor-General of Canada. The two women shared many interests, among them women's rights and reform. Lady Aberdeen had a special interest in Canadian history and invitations to her Rideau Hall events were greatly sought after for their tableaux depicting incidents from Canadian life. During her husband's tenure as Governor-General, she had made it a point to visit every part of the country.

In 1893, Henrietta co-founded the National Council for Women with Lady Aberdeen, a philanthropist who shared Henrietta's passion for social reform. Henrietta served as its chair, for Laws Governing Women and Children for thirty-five years. With the members of the N.C.W., Henrietta worked to improve conditions for three underprivileged female groups in particular. These were prisoners, factory workers and immigrants. Due to their efforts, women were appointed as matrons in the prisons, where conditions were often horrific. The N.C.W. invited other groups across Canada to join hands with them in their struggle for women's rights. One of the groups to join with them was the Dominion Women's Enfranchisement Association, a national organization working towards female suffrage.

Henrietta was very clear about the role of the council in the young country. Rallying the N.C.W. members in a speech she said, "We women of the National Council of Canada as an organized body have work to do and a fitness to do it that no other society in Canada has. The Council, gathering as it does upon its broad platform representatives from all classes of society, from every shade of opinion and religious belief has within itself by united action a power to mould public opinion such as no other society has—a solemn responsibility therefore rests upon us to act, not to talk, to theorize and then go home uninfluenced by the sentiments expressed and listened to.

"So let us not be satisfied with vague results of our council work: giving a little impetus here, a help there to various philanthropic efforts: let us have very clearly defined in our own mind our aim and object; should that not be to develop a noble Canadian womanhood; all our efforts along philanthropic and educational lines being but a means to remove obstacles to that development."

She believed wholeheartedly in the precept that the council had a bigger role to play in the development of Canada. A few gains here and there would not satisfy her.

Around this time, it was becoming apparent that another area in society needed attention. Medical services were desperately required in a rapidly growing country, especially in the rural areas. When Lady Aberdeen visited Vancouver in 1896, she heard stories of how lives of women and children could be saved if they had access to medical services in remote areas. Incidents circulated about how the sick person took a turn for the worse while the male members of the household had gone to fetch medical help from afar.

It was decided at a subsequent N.C.W. meeting in Halifax that a visiting order of nurses be established. While Lady Aberdeen directed operations, it was Henrietta who did all the gruelling detailed work in setting up the Victorian Order of Nurses in 1897. The nurses quickly established stations in major cities of the country, including Ottawa, Montreal, Toronto and Vancouver. From there, nurses travelled to areas where their expertise was much in demand. They offered care to families who earlier had to depend on themselves or on unqualified quacks for their medical needs. Soon more and more hospital V.O.N. sites were established in remote areas. With her background in the studying of Canadian laws, especially with regard to women and children, Henrietta worked with V.O.N. to write bylaws and letters. Lady Aberdeen provided the contacts and Henrietta managed the back of the shop to get this vital organization going.

Duty called Dr. Edwards westwards and the family moved again, this time to Fort McLeod, Alberta, where he was appointed physician of the Blood Reservation. This reserve, nestled between the Belly and St. Mary rivers, was home to four aboriginal groups. Again Henrietta adjusted to life in a different setting, and made it her business to find interest in her surroundings. Being a connoisseur of art, she found the art of the Natives spectacular and built up a valuable collection. Years later, she sold the collection to the University of Alberta, despite a more lucrative offer from institutions in the United States. She had more time to devote to her painting and continued to hone her skills with the brush. Among her prized possessions was a set of china dishes that she had painted for the Chicago World's Fair of 1893. She had requested that she be allowed to keep the collection after the fair was over.

She also made a valuable friend at this time, Frederick Haultain, who was the first premier of the Northwest Territories. With him, she discussed the issues dear to her heart—women's rights and social reform. Henrietta's knowledge of the law helped her write a primer on the legal status of women in Canada. It was published by the government in 1917. She also wrote a similar manual relating to Alberta.

Henrietta Muir Edwards

At the age of 78, in 1927, Henrietta joined with some other women leaders to challenge the *British North American Act*. Nellie McClung, Emily Murphy, Irene Parlby and Louise McKinney banded with Henrietta to start proceedings in the Persons case. That case cemented their names in history. They constituted the Famous Five, playing a pivotal role in Canadian women's history. The case was known as *Edwards vs. Attorney General for Canada*, and Henrietta's role was to do all the practical research and letter-writing involved in such an important endeavour.

Her commitment to female suffrage remained strong through the years. She was in her late seventies, living in Southern Alberta, when she accepted Emily Murphy's invitation to tea in Edmonton to discuss the strategy for the Persons case. As she remarked, "If women had the vote there would be no need to come twice asking for better legislation for women and children, no need to come again and again for the appointment of women inspectors where women and children are employed; we would not ask in vain for the raising of the wage or consent. We do not want to vote as men, we want to vote as women—the more womanly the better."

Henrietta died in Edmonton in 1931 at the age of 82. She is buried beside her husband and son.

Chapter 4
E. Cora Hind

The young woman staring at the scenes flashing past the Canadian Pacific train window was clearly preoccupied as she chewed on her lip while fiddling with her hat. Sitting opposite, her aunt, Alice Hind, looked at her niece with a bemused smile. She was sure Ella Cora Hind had barely noticed that the eastern land of pines and evergreens had long given way to the flatter and distinctive prairie landscape of the west. Her niece had dreams of greatness, reserves of energy and a fearless outlook on life, qualities that the two of them would need in order to survive in a new place. Unused to city life, they were more at home in the rural environment that they had lived in all their lives. It was the challenge of wider opportunities that influenced their decision to come out west.

They were travelling from Grey County, Ontario, and intended to set up home in Winnipeg, a western city; full of opportunities, they had been told by a family member who had moved west. It was 1882 and the first direct train link between eastern Canada to the west had been completed just the previous year. Winnipeg, known as the gateway to the west, was bang in the middle of a boom. They would be sure to find work. Life would be better for them, different from their farm in Ontario, but sure to offer exciting opportunities.

Born in 1861, Ella Cora Hind had been home-schooled by her aunt until a school was built on her grandfather's farm in 1872. She went on to complete her primary education in Flesherton and her higher grades in Orillia. Orphaned at an early age, she went to live with her grandfather and aunt at the farm. It was her grandfather, Joseph Hind, who instilled in her a love for the farming life, agriculture and livestock. Though she didn't know it then, those early lessons on the farm were to form the basis of her career in later years.

At that point however, in 1882, Ella Cora had ambitions of training as a teacher, one of the few professions available to young women at the time. She was confident about the examinations she had taken to qualify as a teacher. The only subject she feared was algebra. Maybe she is pondering on the

E. Cora Hind

outcome of the exams, Alice Hind thought.

Nearing the city of Winnipeg, they looked on in amazement at the quarries, the kilns and busy demeanour of its citizens. In the 1860s, Winnipeg had been but a small frontier town, with wooden residences and a few stores. Its main centre of attraction was the Hudson Bay Post. But by 1881 five thousand people called Winnipeg home, and by five years the number had risen to 20,238. Wheat was now king and the grain industry developed rapidly, bringing change in the lives of the citizenry.

Walking on the city's Main Street was a revelation for Ella Cora and her aunt. Most of the businesses in the city were located on either Main Street or Portage Street. Merchants sold seeds, farming implements and necessities for setting up homesteads. Giant warehouses for the grain business sat alongside the clothing stores while people moved around expertly bypassing the mud and ruts on the streets. It was a far cry from their ordered existence on the family farm in Ontario. The two women soon checked into one of the many hotels that had sprung up near the C.P.R. station.

They decided early on that they would not consider going on to Brandon since it was bound to be backward compared to this vibrant city. They would have a better chance of making a successful transition here in this city, referred to as the Chicago of the North.

Aunt Alice and Ella Cora hired rooms on Dundee Block on Main Street. Alice ran a dressmaking business while Ella Cora impatiently awaited the results of her teacher's exam. She was disappointed when she learned that she had failed the algebra, just as she had feared. Though she was dispirited in the beginning, her aunt encouraged her to study the subject again and retake the exam.

Ella Cora thought about it and decided being a teacher was not the goal in her life. She wanted to be a journalist. It was a bold step for a young woman. She did have a letter of introduction to W. F. Luxton, the owner and editor of the *Winnipeg Free Press*. The newspaper had a big profile in the city and the province, representing the qualities of growth and change that had come to epitomize the city's character. The founding editor, Luxton, and his partner John A. Kenney, had envisaged the growth of their newspaper in tandem with the community that was developing around the Assiniboine and Red rivers. Due to the presence of the railroad, Winnipeg had reincarnated as a boomtown where people from all over the country came to seek a livelihood at the beginning of the new century.

Gathering her courage, she marched up to the offices of the *Winnipeg Free Press* and asked to meet with Luxton. He was pleased to see her, but bluntly told her that the newsroom was no place for a woman. Those days, reporters were hard-smoking and swearing men, there were no separate facilities for women, and covering events through bad weather and worse roads required a strong will and immense physical stamina that women lacked, it was commonly felt. Few women had broken into the citadel that the male-dominated press had erected around itself.

She did not give up, however, and kept revisiting the *Free Press* offices on a fairly regular basis to refresh the editor's memory. In the meantime, Ella Cora decided she needed to work and earn her living. She had recently visited the law offices of Archibald and Howell on some family business, and there she confided to Howell about her inability to make headway in a journalistic career. He suggested she train as a "typewriter." Explaining the new concept, he said that on a recent trip to the United States he had seen a number of young women using these machines in office settings.

Ella Cora applied herself industriously to the new device and in a matter of weeks was able to achieve the requisite speed for employment in the burgeoning city's law office. The law firm of Macdonald, Tupper, Tupper and Dexter employed her at six dollars a week. She was to take the copy from the office manager, which he wrote in a fine copperplate hand, and type it out on her machine. Soon it was her typed briefs that were being read at Winnipeg courts. There were very few "typewriters" in the city.

It was 1893 and she was at her job at the legal firm, which provided her with a steady income, but Ella Cora wasn't content. She knew she had the potential to do much more. That year, she decided to open her own typewriting agency and get business for herself. Her entrepreneurial streak kicked in and she became the province's first public stenographer. In an interview she gave in 1932, she said she worked for all sorts of people in the city—from gold prospectors to diplomats and church officials, learning how people lived and worked.

Her interests were varied and she got involved in the temperance movement in her city through her aunt Alice's work for the W.C.T.U. Ella Cora became an active worker for the W.C.T.U., giving lectures, knocking on doors for people to sign temperance pledges and distributing leaflets, newsletters and posters to inform the public about the Union's goals. The W.C.T.U. performed important services in the areas of domestic violence, abuse and neglect of women and children. At its 1893 provincial convention, the W.C.T.U. adopted a resolution: "that we will never cease our efforts until women stand on equality with men, and have a right to help in forming the laws which govern them both."

At the Winnipeg branch of the W.C.T.U., Ella Cora typed speeches and wrote on social reform herself. She was elected treasurer of the W.C.T.U. and campaigned vigorously about the effects of liquor on householders.

Around this time, Ella Cora became the secretary of the Manitoba Dairy Association. Her innate interest in the agriculture industry was rekindled as she worked closely with farmers and dairy producers. She started writing articles about the industry for various publications in the province. Her specialty became farm affairs, and many of her articles were bylined "E. C. Hind," because editors didn't want readers thinking the articles were written by a woman. She, however, always insisted that her proper signature should be used.

Promoting women's rights was another important activity for Ella Cora. She became involved in the suffrage movement and was one of the founding members of the Manitoba Equal Franchise Association. While she was touring rural areas in the province, she saw first hand how hard life was for farmers and their families. The special problems faced by these farmers included difficulties in combating the fierce prairie weather, in marketing and in storing their crops. Of course there were related issues as well, involving the farm women. Ella Cora found that many of these women were isolated and worked as hard as or harder than the men, even though they had no legal rights as far as the property was concerned. They toiled away on the farms but had to depend on their sons or on other male relatives for any financial matters.

Manitoba had joined the confederation in 1870 and men who owned property got the right to vote. Women were allowed to vote only in certain situations. For instance, from 1887 onwards, they could vote in municipal elections if they owned property. Suffragists like Ella Cora realized early on how important a tool the vote was.

Ella Cora became a familiar name in Winnipeg when she started to accurately predict how big the year's wheat crop in Manitoba would be. She visited wheat farms all over the province, examining crops and calculating values. She checked everything herself and did not depend on existing data. She conducted her own agricultural surveys, in her trademark attire of high boots, buckskin coat, cane and Stetson hat.

In 1898, other authorities predicted that the harvest would be bad. Ella Cora said it would be average. And it was. Her long-cherished dream of combining agriculture and journalism became reality when she was appointed agricultural and commercial editor for the *Winnipeg Free Press* in 1901.

The editors at the paper were vindicated in their choice when, in 1904, American experts declared there would be a much-reduced harvest of thirty-five million bushels, because of black rust. Ella Cora did her own sleuthing and estimated the harvest would be fifty-five million bushels. She proved the other experts wrong: the actual harvest came in at fifty-four million bushels. Her expertise was never again questioned and she became famous for the accuracy of her predictions for close to twenty-nine years. She also analysed livestock breeding, food production and the marketing of crops after harvest. The markets fell or rose on the basis of her predictions, since they had less than a one per cent chance of error. She had started the trend of agricultural reporting, and the *Free Press* devoted a special section to farming and agricultural matters.

Though she was becoming a force to reckon with in the world of agriculture and journalism, Ella Cora remained concerned about the condition of rural women. By 1912, she had become involved with the setting up of Women's Institutes. The core mandate of these institutes was agriculture, family and community work. She helped establish institute branches in both Saskatchewan and Manitoba.

Complete suffrage, applicable to all Manitoba women

only became law in 1916. Ella Cora and other suffragists like Nellie McClung, Amelia Yeomans and Lillian Thomas worked towards their goal of universal female suffrage. In fact, Manitoba was the first province in Canada to give women the right to vote.

Ella Cora was involved in the founding of the Political Equality League in 1912, which actually existed for only four years. Even so, it managed to make its presence felt strongly in the province. From 1912 to 1916 the league campaigned for women's suffrage as a means to set society back on the right path. Later historians have cast aspersions on the mandate since it was largely based on middle-class Anglo-Saxon values and beliefs. It was not a mass movement by any means. Ella Cora and other professional women who worked with the league were fairly well off, educated, and sported the biases of the day. Newer immigrants from other countries found themselves distanced from the league's activities.

Members of the league like Ella Cora were adamant that no violence be used. They were obviously reacting to the militant actions of the British suffragettes. They chose to fight with weapons like satire, speeches and the written word. Their goal was: "stimulate public opinion, by all lawful means."

This type of ideology was termed by scholars as "maternal feminism." Other reform groups working within the province included the W.C.T.U., Trades and Labour

Council and the Grain Growers' Association. There was often an overlapping between these organizations as they collaborated in working toward their reform goals. Ella Cora often gave speeches at the Grain Growers' Association, highlighting the conditions of agricultural workers, particularly women, in Manitoba.

Ella Cora was awarded an honorary L.L.D. by the University of Manitoba and became a life member of the University Women's Club. Retiring from the *Winnipeg Free Press* in 1937, she started travelling the world to observe farming practices. Her book, *My Travels and Findings*, was published in 1939.

Her activities for women's rights didn't slow down after her retirement, however. In a speech at a W.C.T.U. convention, entitled "Progress of Women in Past Fifty Years," she said,

> *It behooves the women of today and especially and particularly university trained women to adopt as their motto— 'What we have we hold' and steadfastly keep this end in view. How can it be done? By your votes. That is the most powerful weapon you can have if you will only use it. Not to put some special party in power but to put into parliaments, legislatures and city*

councils an increasing number of capable and trained women pledged to the sacred duty of seeing women get a square deal.

There is no sex in taxes that I have observed; there is no cut price on beefsteak when a woman buys; doctors charge the same fees for women as men; women pay the same railway fares as men; concert and theatre tickets have no sex marked on them; gas, telephone and electric light cost the same for women as men. Why in heaven's name should this discrimination come in salaries and wages and why should men dare to talk about women invading their fields.

Ella Cora Hind died in October 1942 at the age of 81. The then Canadian prime minister, Mackenzie King, paid his tribute by referring to her as "one of the greatest of Canadian women."

Chapter 5
Irene Parlby

Lately, the heavily-furnished Victorian rooms at her family home in London, England, had seemed stuffier than usual to Irene Marryat. She thought back to the days when she lived in India during the late 1800s. Her father, Colonel Ernest Lindsay Marryat, was manager of the Bengal and North Western Railways and the family was stationed in Rawalpindi. This was the biggest cantonment occupied by the British in South Asia. Since her father was an official of importance, life for Irene and her five sisters was one of leisure and fun.

It was a life she loved—the sense of adventure was

always prominent in Irene from the beginning. She had a pony named Medley. There were horse races with her sisters (with the grooms looking on), small hills they climbed, forested paths they explored and waterfalls they bathed in. During the evenings at home, they wrote, produced and put on plays for their family and visiting friends. As they climbed up steep hillsides and wandered among the pine forests, Irene must have hoped fervently that life would continue in the same vein.

Even years later, she never forgot the trip her family made to Agra to see the Taj Mahal. The splendour and symmetry of that marble monument to love made an indelible impression on her mind. All things come to an end, however, and Colonel Marryat retired when Irene was sixteen and the family had to leave India and return to a more mundane existence in England. Her father had his own dream that he wanted to fulfill. He bought land and cattle and started a new life as a farmer. He also involved himself in philanthropic projects in the area. What a change in environment it was for young Irene and her sisters! There were very few people in the area, no young people their age, not even a church to relieve the isolation.

Poor Irene found it very hard to adjust to life in provincial England and began to pine for more exciting times. She went to Germany to study piano, but was still unsatisfied. Her father noticed the change and asked her if she would

Irene Parlby, with other members of the Alberta legislature

like to study medicine at university. It was an unusual step for Colonel Marryat to take. Few women attended university in those days, but he was seriously concerned about his daughter. But Irene was more interested in writing and drama than medicine. Instead, she got together with her family and put up a production of Oliver Goldsmith's *She Stoops to Conquer*. The production was more ambitious than usual and was deemed a great success. The proceeds went to the Philanthropic Farm School for Boys, a project that Colonel Marryat was interested in. It was such a success that they were asked for a repeat performance at the neighbouring town and more money was raised.

It was soon time for Irene's formal "coming out" in London. As she watched her mother and sisters fretting over the taffeta and tulle gowns, the jewels and the shoes, she decided she wanted more out of life than a stultifying round of parties. The constraints of the Victorian period, with its strict rules about what women could and could not do, were wearing her down. She did enjoy some of the partying, but it wasn't an all-consuming passion for her. What she really wanted was a career in acting; but that was not a possibility at all considering her parents' respectable families. It just wasn't socially acceptable. The Marryats were from an old family, established since 1066. Her father's relatives were all placed in responsible positions in the country's administration and her mother came from the Lynch family, from prominent Irish stock. Naturally, any career carrying the slightest whiff of something outside the ordinary was frowned upon.

In 1896, things took an interesting turn for Irene. A friend of her parents from Rawalpindi days, Mrs. Alice Westhead, came visiting, and Irene was mesmerized by what the guest had to say. Mrs. Westhead was on her way back to the Buffalo Lake District in Canada's West. Asked to describe her life there, she told tales of the new country's Northwest Territories, of the buffalo herds, the open spaces and the bands of Natives. Irene was hooked into the romance of active frontier life. All her love for adventure, simmering inside the restrictive life of a single Victorian woman with no particular education or career, bubbled up.

Seeing young Irene's enthusiasm, Mrs. Westhead invited her to visit the ranch and see for herself the life of a rancher in Canada's Northwest Territories. Irene accepted with great joy and started on a journey to Canada. This journey would have momentous consequences.

Her intention was to "make herself useful" on the ranch and, in the process, see as much as possible of life in the West.

She saw first hand the hard work that cowboys put into the ranch. Irene realized how connected with nature one must be in order to run a ranch successfully. The cattle involved lots of work, as did the horses. At the Westhead ranch, Irene learned the basics of returning to nature and savoured the taste of an adventurous life, a far cry from the boring slowness of Victorian customs and manners that she had been chafing under.

But her life was about to change even more. She met Walter Parlby, an Englishman educated in Oxford, ranching in the province. The local town had originally been named Toddsville, after Joseph Todd, from Michigan, who was travelling in the area. He and his family stopped there and had found the quality of the grass, water and soil excellent. Later, though, the President of the Canadian Pacific Railway renamed the town Alix after the first woman settler, Mrs. Alexia Westhead.

The Westheads owned the only big house in the town and it was at their house that Irene met young Walter Parlby, a classics scholar, at a social event in 1896. Walter was also an old India hand, having worked at a tea plantation in Assam for three years. They had a lot in common and discussed their love for India to their heart's content. They married in March at the Westhead home. The Parlbys were one of the first families to set up home in Alix. They named their home Dartmoor and indulged in the open spaces, the scenery and their garden. In 1899, a son, Humphrey, was born to Irene and Walter.

By 1913, Irene was becoming more interested in cooperative movements and was taking an active part in community life in Alix. The catalyst had been a Miss Jean Reed, who came to the area to work as a housekeeper at the nearby Marryat household. A Scot educated in England, Miss Reed boasted radical notions about feminism and was happiest expounding her ideas to the people around her. Earlier, she had been an associate of the famous English suffragette Emmeline Pankhurst in London. Miss Reed had even taken a prominent role in the English suffragettes' militant activities.

Her talks spurred the imagination of women in the area, specially Irene. Over cups of tea, they pondered the exciting life that Miss Reed had lived in London, courting arrest with her militant colleagues. Emmeline Pankhurst and her daughters Christabel and Sylvia had created a stir in London in demanding suffrage rights. They employed daring tactics which included stone throwing, loud demonstrations and hunger strikes.

Irene was absorbed by the ideas of equality and suffrage that Miss Reed spoke so passionately about. She could see that the conditions of some of the farm women in the province needed to be addressed. Many of the women lived and worked on the family farms for their entire lives, suffering from exhaustion and isolation. New immigrants kept arriving and, with the advent of the railways in the West, things were changing rapidly. Most of the women barely had any recreation, and educational opportunities for them were limited. Their minds were not broadened and therefore the children they raised also suffered. Reading material was nonexistent and there was no effort being made by anyone to improve the rural women's lives.

A friend of Miss Reed's from London, Mrs. Elizabeth Mitchell, visited her at Alix around this time. Mrs. Mitchell was on a tour of Canada to see what kind of women's organizations existed, the participation of the populace and the issues they addressed. She found the largely rural-centred women's base in Alix ready for change, and suggested that the area's women could meet in the town to establish a club for social congress. Most of the women were farm women and welcomed this exciting initiative, which promised an addition to their otherwise drab social lives. The Alix Women's Country Club was formed in 1913. Leona Barritt was elected president and Irene became the secretary.

This event marked the beginning of Irene's public life, historians believe. She found herself drawn to the farm women and their set of issues, and one of her first initiatives was to found a library. Irene herself was an avid reader and she realized that there was a lack of reading material in the community. She believed that reading would open doors for many of the farm women. But there was the problem of books. Who would be willing to buy books for the new library?

With typical tenacity, Irene advertised in London's *Spectator*, requesting books for the new library at Alix. Readers could mail in any books they could spare. This resulted in readers' sending off a generous amount of books, and soon the library became a reality. Farm women came from neighbouring areas on afternoons, riding horses or in buggies, and borrowed reading material, thus ensuring the start of many a life-long affair with books. Many women in the club thanked Irene for her efforts in setting up the library. At the end of long work-filled days on the prairie, when the children were asleep and the kitchen silent, many a farmer's wife relaxed with a book with her feet up. Some of their isolation was reduced and they looked forward to the club meetings and the promise of a long chat and a book to take home.

Meanwhile, on another front, Irene's idea of involving women in community life received a boost. A few years earlier, the United Farmers of Alberta had been established in the province as a cooperative movement dedicated to the interests of farmers. Walter Parlby was the president. Farmers had realized that they could do better as a collective than they could as individuals. The organization gained support among the rural population and slowly started becoming more active in the politics of the province. One of its goals was equal rights for women.

The U.F.A. floated its convention in 1915. The Alix Women's Country Club was invited, but, since Irene was ill with the flu, Miss Reed and Mrs. Barritt attended. The following year, Irene was elected president of the U.F.A.'s Women's Auxiliary. She proposed that the Women's Auxilliary become a distinct organization, linked to, but separate from, the U.F.A. Henry Wise Wood was the U.F.A. president at the time, and the motion, proposed by Irene, was carried. The new organization was called the United Farm Women of Alberta. At the convention, she presented a paper, "Women's Place in the Nation," that clearly stated her views that women needed to be more active in society.

Irene and Mrs. Barritt travelled all over the province that

year to gauge the issues facing women in the smaller hamlets and towns. They travelled by coach, wagons and buggies, staying at local homes and farms, convening meetings for the farmwomen and setting up chapters of the U.F.W.A. At the end of four years, the U.F.W.A. had almost four thousand members, in 293 chapters all over the province.

Irene's public role was not limited to work for the U.F.W.A. She was also involved in the public health system. She was the municipal health convenor and sat on a committee to draft a bill for the setting up of municipal hospitals. The *Municipal Hospitals Act* drafted by the committee was passed in 1919. Irene was a strong proponent of travelling dental and medical clinics, and of public health nurses. Given the prairie distances and the limited resources, these were two very forward-thinking ideas.

It was 1921 and she was nominated by the U.F.A. to stand as a provincial candidate for Lacombe. She was reluctant to do so, largely because she did not like the rudeness and heckling that went with political campaigns. She did agree in the end, but later in life remembered it as being a rough time for her. It took a great deal of effort to stand up to the harassment. Though she spoke clearly and had decided views on her causes, she was subjected to a lot of verbal abuse. She exclaimed ruefully at one point, "The only thing which seemed to concern my opponents was that I am a woman—and worse, an Englishwoman who, although

I came to Western Canada when it was still an undeveloped wilderness, could not possibly know anything about it!"

To her great surprise, she won the election and credited the farmers for her victory. The U.F.A. was a force to reckon with in the Alberta legislature, with the majority of seats. She represented Lacombe for fourteen years and had a good innings as Minister Without Portfolio. During her long tenure, she pushed for the reform that she so strongly believed in—travelling clinics for the rural areas, distance education and the uplifting of women's lives. In 1925, she successfully followed through with the *Minimum Wage for Women Act*. This was the first time in the country that women would be guaranteed a minimum wage in the workplace.

According to the law, the minimum was such that it would be possible for working women to earn enough to "preserve their health, morals and efficiency." Women were still not eligible for vacation pay or for other benefits, and their economic condition remained precarious, but Irene had set the ball rolling by bringing some parity into the lives of working women.

Under a U.F.A. government initiative, she travelled to Denmark and Sweden to study educational institutions and cooperative movements there. The difficulty in rural areas where illiteracy was rampant was that parents were unwilling to spare children to go to school since it took them away from their chores on the farm. It was her job to work out a suitable model which would enable students to combine their farming duties with basic education.

She was also involved by this time in the Persons case, along with the other four women who would achieve international fame through this landmark legislation.

In 1930, Prime Minister R. B. Bennet asked that she visit the Assembly of Nations in Geneva, representing Canada. In a speech there, she voiced her opinions about integration of immigrants into society. One of the ways this could be achieved, she suggested, was through the citizenship ceremonies that continue even today. Her ideas on multiculturalism still form the basis of many newer government policies.

However, while returning from Geneva, Irene fell ill and was advised by her doctor to give up her strenuous public activities. She continued her political engagements for a while, but eventually, in 1944, she retired. Irene subsequently led a quiet life in Dartmoor, her home on Parlby Lake, and died at the age of 97.

Chapter 6
Louise McKinney

The church was overflowing with black-clad mourners. There was barely room to stand at the church in Claresholm, Alberta, on that warm July afternoon in 1931. All the attendees carried small white ribbons in their hands. Bunches of white lilies filled the vases. Women and men came from all over the country as well as from abroad to honour the memory of the deceased. One of the Alberta's ablest had passed away. It hardly seemed possible—it was only a few days ago that Mrs. Louise McKinney had presided over the Women's Christian Temperance Union national meeting in Toronto.

There she was elected vice-president of the organization. This was a fitting tribute to the woman who had devoted her entire life to working for the W.C.T.U. She had believed whole heartedly in the goals of temperance and the necessity of educating the general public about the effects of alcohol on the human system. Louise McKinney was instrumental in establishing W.C.T.U. branches all over the country.

Mourners also recalled her energy and tireless resolve in working for the suffrage movement. The organ pealed its mournful cadence as all present reflected on the life and legacy of Louise McKinney. Her family accepted condolences with a sense of bewilderment. It seemed as if there was yet so much left for Mrs McKinney to do. Her unfinished work would now have to be carried on by others, they realized.

Yet, they recalled how she had spoken to a friend after returning from the convention: "The other world seems nearer and more real when so many of earth's loved ones are there, and it comes to matter little whether it is a place or condition—we know it is prepared for those who love Him and those who serve Him here will continue to serve Him throughout Eternity."

When her coffin was lowered into the hallowed ground, the mourners filed past. Each dropped a small white ribbon onto the coffin. Hundreds of white ribbons soon filled up the space. One could be sure Mrs. McKinney was reassured by this show of support. She would take it that her life's work would carry on. What did the white ribbons represent? What was the significance of those tiny bits of fabric?

The white ribbon bows symbolized purity and faith, in the W.C.T.U. parlance. Mrs. McKinney had been passionately devoted to this cause for over forty years. Through her work at the W.C.T.U., she ventured into the territory of women's enfranchisement. As one of the leading players in the Persons case, Louise McKinney's activism extended to include property rights for Canadian women too.

Her pioneering spirit was apparent from the beginning when she started life as Louise Crummy in 1868 at a farm in Frankville, Ontario. Hers was a Methodist family, with seven brothers and three sisters and their parents, Richard and Esther Crummy. With her siblings, she graduated from Athens High School. Later, she went on to Ottawa Normal School, training to be a teacher.

By 1886 she was teaching at a school in the Frankville area. Schoolhouses in those days were simple affairs of logs, with a big box stove in the middle. Teachers' duties included not only educating their young pupils in the three Rs (reading, writing and arithmetic) but also filling the oil lamps and cleaning the lamps' chimneys. Women teachers were not allowed to marry. As teacher, she sometimes made a big pot of stew on the stove and lunched with her pupils on cold winter days.

Louise had initially wanted to become a doctor but, being a pragmatist, realized how difficult it was for women to be admitted to medical schools. That was a fight waiting to be fought. Instead, she desired to make a difference and chose the teaching profession to achieve her goal. She didn't bemoan what she couldn't have, but moved ahead with what she did—that was a characteristic that would stand her in good stead throughout her life. In the next four years, Louise taught in many of the area schools. The villages were settlements, mostly, with hard-working pioneering families building the schoolhouses themselves. If there was no schoolhouse, the lessons were conducted in a settler's home, the general store or the village church.

One of Louise's married sisters lived in Drayton, North Dakota. It, too, was a pioneer settlement and boasted of the Red River of the North, where catfish thrived. Louise went for a visit to her sister and was charmed by the place. She accepted a position at the school there and taught for three years. Joining the W.C.T.U. chapter in Drayton proved to be a big step in Louise's life. In 1894, at the age of 26, she was made the union organizer. Her industry and passion for the W.C.T.U. cause had obviously been noticed.

Another event of great importance occurred at this time. She met an Irishman named James McKinney. Their common background included Irish descent and an attachment to Canada. James came from a small community

Louise McKinney

near Ottawa and was also a strong believer in the temperance cause. They married in Frankville in 1896 in the Crummy family homestead.

The young couple went back to Drayton and settled down to farm. A son, Willard, was born. He was named after Frances Willard, an American temperance activist and suffragist, and one of the founders of the W.C.T.U. Being a mother did not slow Louise's activities with the W.C.T.U. She travelled to many neighbouring hamlets to set up W.C.T.U. chapters. The organization established reading rooms and shelters for women workers.

It was a job she thrived in. Louise and her colleagues promoted the ideas of morality, a healthy family life, sobriety in society and prohibition. The W.C.T.U. has been called "the first women's mass movement," by Ruth Bordin in *Woman*

Louise McKinney

and Temperance: The Quest for Power and Liberty, 1873-1900 (Philadelphia: Temple University Press, 1981).

With charismatic and able leaders like Louise McKinney, women joined the W.C.T.U. in huge numbers. Though temperance was their main thrust, the W.C.T.U. program involved a broader understanding of women's place in society. By the late 1870s, the W.C.T.U. began to adopt a more political approach in their agenda. In 1898, Louise was elected as the First District president. She attended the silver jubilee national convention of the W.C.T.U. in Seattle the following year.

But things were changing for the young McKinney family. Canada, with its vast prairie land, family ties and the need for reform lured them back. They answered a call to return to their Canadian roots. In 1903, Louise and her family moved to a new town in the prairies of the Canadian West—Claresholm, in southern Alberta. (The province was, at that time, still part of the Northwest Territories. Alberta and Saskatchewan became provinces in the Dominion of Canada only two years later, in 1905.)

Fertile land was plentiful in Claresholm, but there was certainly much to be done. There was no church established and Louise, with her characteristic energy, soon set about rectifying that lack. Both James and Louise helped in the building of the first Methodist church in Claresholm. Louise was more directly involved in establishing the W.C.T.U.

branch in the town. She was elected the first president of the W.C.T.U. chapter there and held that post for the next twenty-five years. That meant plenty of travelling in inclement weather, leaving her family behind, speaking at podiums in small prairie towns where few women turned up to hear her. But she was indefatigable and continued her crusade. She set up almost forty chapters of the W.C.T.U. in different parts of the provinces of Alberta and Saskatchewan.

It was common to see Louise McKinney travelling summer and winter over distances by buggy or the smoke-belching railway, alighting in the small towns where she often met with indifference or hostility from the inhabitants. Some men joked that W.C.T.U. actually stood for Women Continually Torment Us. But the W.C.T.U. was really at the heart of the women's movement in Canada. Louise never let the people she addressed forget that temperance did not only refer to drink. It was a way of life, with emphasis on Christian values. She had a deep-seated force of conviction about her work with its pro-family bias. She advocated the setting up of temperance legions in schools to inculcate temperance principles in youth.

Louise was active in many other aspects of life in her town. She led the Ladies Aid and the Woman's Missionary Society as well. She led a full public life and it was perhaps inevitable that she become involved in politics. Already war clouds were hanging over Europe—it was 1914. This affected

Canada as well, as part of the British Empire. Men were recruited to the war effort and there were serious shortages in the Canadian labour market. The women's movement was affected. More women worked outside their homes and they demanded a say in their own affairs.

Alberta became the second province to enforce prohibition, in 1915. Louise McKinney played a big role in the processing of this legislation. She believed in continuous education where temperance matters were concerned. She promoted the work done by the Loyal Temperance Legions with its Certificate of Membership. The certificate was a pledge that members signed, and gave reasons why temperance was necessary in a civic and truly Christian life. Later historians have condemned these early feminists' proselytizing approach, but they were the largely white, middle-class Protestant backbone of the nascent Canadian women's movement.

In 1916, women in Alberta won the right to vote. They could also stand for legislative office. It was natural for a public-spirited person like Louise to run as a candidate in the 1917 provincial elections. She was disgusted with the nexus that thrived between liquor interests and the political parties. The companies contributed heavily to political party funds. In this she was joined by Nellie McClung.

Louise's idealistic nature did not allow her to accept this status quo. She became a candidate for the Non Partisan

League in the constituency of Claresholm. She won the election as an independent candidate on the prohibition platform. Besides being an important milestone for her, her entry into politics allowed Louise to vigorously promote the two causes dear to her heart—temperance and women's rights. She was dissatisfied with both existing parties in the political landscape, the Conservatives and the Liberals. Just like thousands of Albertans, she felt that neither of these parties truly represented the interests of their basically agrarian province.

Louise McKinney has the distinction of being the first woman to be sworn in to a legislature in Canada, and indeed, to any legislature in the British Empire. She wrote, "In the office where we were sworn in and signed the roll, the men welcomed us and made us feel that they were honoured in being members of the legislative body that was making history…in all the days that followed we were accepted as a matter of fact and as though we had a perfect right to be there, and one almost forgot that there was anything new in the situation."

McKinney was a strong debater and put forth her views on various subjects forcefully in the provincial legislature. She introduced issues like strict liquor control laws and measures to safeguard the interests of widows and women with particular reference to homesteads and property. Her commitment to women's rights was growing stronger as she realized the dire straits that some women were thrown into after the male patriarchs dealt their hands.

She introduced a motion for the eventual passing of the *Dower Act*. This meant that a certain portion of a deceased husband's property went to the widow so she would not have to depend on the charity of male family members. It also put a stop to the current law which decreed a man could sell or mortgage the property without the woman's knowledge. Naturally this was a huge step towards reducing the disparity existing for women then.

Financial independence was an important part of women's rights, Louise had realized early on. In 1919, she said, "Since many women will either from choice or from force of circumstances continue to earn a living outside the home, are we not duty-bound to stand for the principle of equal pay for equal work?" Her foresight seems amazing if compared to current circumstances many decades later. Pay equity is still a hotly debated issue in modern Canada. Systemic failures still plague the labour market with regard to wages, even though Canadian women have come a long way since Louise McKinney's time.

Part of the problem stems from the distinction between the "worthiness" of men's work as opposed to that of women. In an article published in the *Canadian Home Journal* in August 1919, Louise discussed what constituted women's work and how Canadians were to adapt to the new conditions of life after war. Long before modern feminists debated the schism between a man's world and woman's, Louise was aware of the need to validate women's lives in terms of the enormous workload they carried.

"Woman's work and woman's sphere have always furnished a favourite topic of conversation. Her activities and resourcefulness during the war exploded many of the old theories and gained for her many of the privileges which for years she had claimed to be her right. Now that the war is over the public mind is seized with a new dread, and the subject for popular comment is whether women will be willing to relinquish her newfound liberty and wider sphere of activity and resume her place as home-maker in the same old way or will she continue to claim her present place in the industrial world and thus constitute one more of the already numerous after-the-war problems. What, after all, is the purpose of woman's life? The purpose of woman's life is just the same as the purpose of man's life—that she may make the best possible contribution to the generation in which she is living."

Louise McKinney's confidence in Canadian women's abilities to strike a balance between life at home and outside her home never wavered. Even though she lost the election in 1921, she continued her work with the United Farmers of Alberta (U.F.A.), which absorbed the smaller Non Partisan League. She did not run for office again.

By 1927, she was involved in the Persons case. It was

a historic case, fought tooth and nail by the Famous Five, of which Louise was a member. They took on the Canadian establishment, going right up to the Privy Council in Britain to have Canadian women declared as persons under the law. This had enormous implications for the women's movement, as it allowed women to be eligible for appointment to the Senate and to serve in federal governments.

Her commitment to the W.C.T.U. cause did not waver. She attended the national conference in 1931, returning home to Claresholm where she took ill suddenly. She died at her home on July 10 at 63 years of age.

Chapter 7
Emily Murphy

Edmonton's courthouse was fuller than ever that day in 1916. After all, people are the same everywhere, thirsting for salacious gossip and scandal. For days before that morning, there had been considerable talk about the upcoming trial. Men snickered and winked amongst themselves; women shook their heads and whispered behind their hands. There was an air of expectation, of titillation. Wholly unnecessary, thought Emily Murphy, of Edmonton's Local Council of Women. The trial involved some prostitutes who were arrested under "questionable circumstances" in the city's seedier streets.

People had come out for a fun time at the courthouse. Emily had no doubt the stories of the court proceedings would be related over and over again to friends and drinking partners in the saloons and bars of Edmonton. She looked at the women on the stand, huddled together, noting their cheap clothes, lavish hairdos and garish makeup inciting comment and laughter in the packed courtroom. She felt pity stirring her heart and anger that these women were being gawked at so openly. But the climax was yet to come.

The presiding judge surveyed the court and made his remarks. Emily Murphy and her group of friends from the Local Council of Women were stunned. They had just been ejected from the court, because the judge deemed that the proceedings would be too scandalous and "not fit for mixed company."

Outraged at the judge's pronouncement, Emily became determined not to let the matter drop. "If the evidence is not fit to be heard in mixed company," she wrote, "then... the government must set up a special court presided over by women, to try other women." Her resolve strengthened the more she delved into the issue and garnered the support of her colleagues at the Local Council. She requested a meeting with the attorney general of Alberta, A. W. Cross, and presented him with a petition to establish a woman's criminal court, to be presided over by a woman.

Soon after, much to her surprise, the provincial Liberal

Emily Murphy

government under Arthur Sifton appointed her the first female judge. Emily Murphy holds the distinction of being the first woman to be appointed a judge anywhere in the British Commonwealth of Nations. The post of police magistrate was one of great responsibility and no sooner had the announcement been made than hundreds of congratulatory messages began to pour into the Murphy residence and the Local Council offices. It was a great moment for the burgeoning women's movement in Canada.

Emily Murphy was not going to rest on her laurels, however. She launched her judicial career with serious reading on court procedure and law. Her background did prove to be a big help. Emily came from a family of lawyers. Born in 1868 in Cookstown, Ontario, Emily Fergusson had a privileged childhood on her father's property about sixty miles to the north of Toronto. Nicknamed "Sunshine," Emily lived with her five siblings on an estate with ponies, and plenty of activities like tree-climbing, fishing and cricket. Her father was an Irishman who had arrived on Canadian shores at the age of twelve with his widowed mother and five siblings. On Emily's mother's side her grandfather, Ogle R. Gowan, had been a member of the government of Upper Canada, as well as the founder and grandmaster of the Orange Order in Canada.

Childhood for Emily was marked by a great deal of fun and play-acting. She performed plays as a child for such distinguished company as Sir John A. Macdonald and Sir Charles Tupper, at the Fergusson home. Three of her brothers went on to become lawyers, one, a doctor—her lawyer brothers were to prove beneficial to her later in life.

Though she didn't formally qualify as a lawyer, she did become a legal expert through her voluminous reading and her growing experience. But all that came later. At fifteen, Emily was enrolled as a boarder at Toronto's exclusive Bishop Strachan School for Girls. This school aimed at taking the cream of Toronto's students and creating leaders. It was a novel concept in a time when girls were very much expected to be mere subsidiaries to the male population. Higher education for girls was stressed and the idea that girls were meant only to be social butterflies was frowned upon by the progressive people who ran that school. Not surprisingly, Emily was deeply influenced by the series of lady principals who headed the school, each of whom intended to turn girls and women into useful members of society. Emily was to be homesick for the life she had before her time at the boarding school, but gradually she grew to love the school's environment, too. She had a good memory, and that served her well in her academic pursuits.

During her time at the school, two of her brothers came visiting, bringing along with them a young friend named Arthur Murphy. Studying to be an Anglican minister, Arthur, though eleven years her senior, instantly fell in love with Emily. Though the school rules were very strict, Emily and Arthur met often and decided to marry once she had graduated. They had a fashionable wedding in Toronto when she turned nineteen and was out of school, setting up home near Lake Simcoe.

Emily's life changed with the responsibilities that came with being the wife of a minister. She participated willingly in the community, organizing bazaars and Bible classes, while taking over the presidency of the missionary society. These duties helped prepare her for her future career as a key player in women's rights issues on the nation's stage. Though she was a very young woman at the time, she learned how to work with people of differing temperaments, to keep an eye on the bigger picture, and to feel genuine sympathy for those less fortunate than her. All these traits were to go towards the development of the strong-willed woman who later became a police magistrate and a judge.

Emily became the mother of four daughters. Due to the nature of her husband's job, they moved all over the province, from Chatham to Ingersoll. In Ingersoll, she was in her twenty-fifth year, strong and independent, with decided ideas about her responsibilities. She had matured in her ideas and this intellectual development showed in the way she conducted herself when a controversial topic arose. Whether or not women were capable of taking on administrative duties in the church generated an intense debate among the congregation. She was of the opinion that women could accept the responsibilities within the church without compromising her home affairs. She argued that, "...women could contribute much to the administrative body of the church." Her interest in women's rights and the issues that affected them had grown stronger by this time. Yet she found herself on a lonely road. There were few supporters on whom she could count to further her views. It was a taxing time for her but it contributed to her developing courage to live by her convictions.

During this time, Arthur was asked to become a missionary in Ontario and the family spent the next two years in various small-town parishes. She had already started writing by then, keeping a diary to record her experiences. Social conditions among the poorer sections of Ontario's population were quite bad and Emily kept track of what she witnessed, thinking she might later write articles about what she had seen. Industrialization was steadily taking hold, and people were moving from their farms to the towns.

This was about the time when the public systems of health, social security and education, as we know them today, were just beginning. Though their full development was still a few years away, the seeds of the trade union movement were being sown in the factories. Workers contributed to funds that served as insurance in case of emergencies like sudden illnesses, accidents or death. Emily noted and recorded all this in her diaries.

In 1898, the Murphys were offered a chance to travel to England for a year. It was a chance to preach there, and Arthur accepted. On the voyage, however, Emily had to learn to ignore the patronizing attitudes of the British and American travellers towards Canadians. She made up her mind to write under the name of "Janey Canuck." That would be her salute towards the country of her birth.

Emily and her family were stationed in various parts of England. They lived for some time in both Liverpool and the East End of London, where she discovered, to her horror, the pathetic conditions of the poorer sections of the population.

She found that the problems of prostitution and poverty were even greater than in her own country. By the time the year ended they were ready to get back to Canada. She wrote ecstatically, "...once more in the first, best country, God's fairest gift to man—the land of the Maple".

The Murphy family settled down in Toronto and Emily had her first book published. *The Impressions of Janey Canuck Abroad* achieved much success in both England and Canada, turning her into a celebrity author. *The National Monthly of Canada* asked her to become a regular contributor. She later became a woman's editor for that periodical. It marked the end of an era when Queen Victoria died, and the new century began. The Victorian period was officially over, bringing in the more fun-loving Edwardians at the helm. But for Emily, things took a turn for the worse. Her husband Arthur fell ill with the dreaded typhoid. Emily, and then her daughter Doris, also caught the disease. Though Emily and Arthur recovered, six-year-old Doris did not, and the heart-broken parents had to live through the difficult days after her untimely demise. It became a chore for Emily to get by from day to day, with the grief festering in her heart. Arthur was taking longer to recover and the doctors said a move to a different climate was imperative.

They moved to Swan River in northwestern Manitoba, about thirty miles north of Winnipeg. The Murphys had earlier invested in some land in Swan River, so it made sense to move there. Emily was fascinated by her first glimpse of the West. "How the sun shines here in Winnipeg!" she wrote. "One drinks it in like wine. And how the bells ring! It is a town of bells and light set in a blaze of gold. Surely the West is golden—the Sky, flowers, wheat, hearts."

They loved Winnipeg's up-and-coming character, its air of business and enterprise. They also became aware of the number of immigrants who thronged the streets of the city.

"On the streets of Winnipeg, there are people who smile at you in English, but speak in Russian. There are rushful, pushful people from 'the States', stiff-tongued Germans, ginger-headed Icelanders, Galacians, Norwegians, Poles and Frenchmen, all of whom are rapidly becoming irreproachably Canadian. In all, there are sixty tongues in the pot," Emily declared in admiration. An appreciation of what it was to be truly Canadian, living in harmony with people from all over the world, took root in Emily at this time.

However, it wasn't to be all fun. The Murphys were not to settle in Winnipeg but had to travel two days onward to Swan Lake. After the bustle of Winnipeg, it was a severe disappointment to realize how isolated Swan Lake was.

By 1906, the Murphys had moved again, to Edmonton. There Emily started taking up the causes dear to her heart. The laws in Alberta at the time decreed that a husband could dispose of his property without the consent of his spouse, and he was not obliged to give her any of the proceeds. This often left many women destitute after years of working on the family farm. Emily decided to address this issue head-on when she came into contact with a woman who was abandoned when her husband sold off the farm and rendered her penniless, dependent on the charity of relatives and strangers.

Emily kicked off a campaign to remedy this injustice. Her plan of action was to gather the facts, write articles and apply to the provincial legislature to protect the rights of women. She did not taste success immediately. The *Dower Act* generated a tough fight in the provincial legislature and it was only in 1911 that the Alberta legislature finally passed the bill, but it did stipulate that one third of the property of the husband was to be awarded to his spouse.

During this time she was also embarking on a literary journey. She completed her second book, *Janey Canuck in the West*, and accepted the position of editor at the *Winnipeg Telegram*. Her social instincts well-honed by now, she investigated the conditions at a local hospital, filing a brutally honest report to the hospital board—of which she was a member. She became president of the Canadian Women's Press Club and had two more books published.

In 1911, she befriended Emmeline Pankhurst, the British militant suffragette, who was on a North American tour. She also made friends with Nellie McClung, and became a passionate advocate of women's rights and enfranchisement.

They fought the fight together, and by 1916 Alberta became the third province in Canada to give the vote to women.

However, this was also the year in which Emily became the first female judge in the British Commonwealth. She spent her days preparing for this august experience by brushing up her knowledge about court procedure and law. She claimed that her first days at the court as a judge were, "as pleasant an experience as running rapids without a guide."

She ran into some stormy weather on the first day itself. The defence counsel, Eardley Jackson, argued that Emily could not hear the case because she was not "a person" in the eyes of the law. Though Jackson had a legal point in his favour, Emily knew that a struggle to change the status quo was coming in the future. Her judicial career was marked by many instances of such harassment. However, she was not at all biased towards female offenders.

Emily continued to engage in social issues, paramount among them being narcotic trafficking. She wrote articles on the subject in *Macleans* that were published in book form in 1922 as *The Black Candle*. Controversially, Emily also advocated a form of eugenics, which promoted sterilization of "the mentally deficient". She ran into a lot of criticism from later feminist scholars and historians on account of her views.

Emily is best remembered for her work on the Persons case. Along with four other Canadian women, she fought for the right to have women legally declared to be "persons," so that they could be appointed senators and have a say in the running of their country.

She retired in 1931, and passed away two years later at her Edmonton home.

Chapter 8
Nellie McClung

A prairie picnic day in Manitoba in July 1883 meant lots of excitement for the hard-working settlers assembled at Tiger Hills, Millford, where the Souris river meets the waters of the Assiniboine. In the sunshine, masses of orange lilies and sweet brier roses nodded, and the Saskatoon berries were just beginning to ripen. Neighbours were in a good mood as they surveyed the tables set by the river simply groaning with food—plates piled high with raisin buns, doughnuts, hard-boiled eggs, lettuce smothered in sour cream and mustard. Chocolates from Brandon, thirty-five miles away, were the highlight of the spread, however, and there were many covetous glances cast in the direction of the wooden pail where they reposed.

Ten-year old Nellie looked wonderingly at her mother and the way her hair framed her usually solemn face. Letitia Mooney had taken off her hat and was chatting with the other farm women who were minding babies. The men were assembled in a group under the poplar trees, and with their pipes in their mouths were discussing the reasons they had moved west.

Many of the settlers had moved in from Ontario. The Mooney family had farmed earlier in Grey County, Ontario. It was a tough life, with the stony soil making for back-breaking labour. Mooney and his family cursed the heavy effort involved, and managed to eke out an existence only with difficulty. The Mooneys were among the almost forty thousand people who moved west between 1876 and 1881.

The general atmosphere of fun at the picnic was further stoked by the prospect of games. The young people had drawn up a list of activities, among them a "slow ox" race and baseball games. Nellie was wild with enthusiasm as she surveyed Jake, their black and white ox, competing in the slow ox race. In such a "race," each man would ride a neighbour's ox, rather than his own. The rider would try to convince the ox he was riding to move down the course quickly, but the rule was that no whips, spurs or beatings could be used in egging the animals on. The slowest ox—the one that best

Nellie McClung (right) and Emmeline Pankhurst

resisted his rider's encouragement—would win.

She was standing in a copse of trees with Mrs. Daly's baby in a carriage, hoping that Jake would win. The race began and, despite all the cheering and shouting, Jake moved at a leisurely pace. Then, suddenly, he reared up like a wild thing, snorted with rage, and galloped furiously towards Nellie and the baby. She was too frozen to react and the air was filled with horrified screams as the picnickers realized what was happening. Jake was bellowing with pain and they saw the blood spurting from his sides. Providentially, Jake swerved at the last second and crashed into the bushes. He was wounded and bleeding heavily.

The truth came out. The man riding him had been drinking and had used spurs on Jake. That episode spoiled the picnic. It also cast its long shadow throughout Nellie's life.

"I remember a good day spoiled; peaceful neighbours suddenly growing quarrelsome, and feel again a helpless blinding fear, and see blood dyeing the side of a dumb beast," wrote Nellie in her autobiography, *Clearing in the West.*

Nellie was to become a committed temperance activist throughout her life and she never forgot that early introduction to the evils of drink.

Born in 1873, Nellie Mooney was the quintessential farm girl who helped her family in their daily chores, which included milking the cows, making soap, sewing, baking and cooking. However, her parents insisted that she have an education as well, and all her sisters were students at Northfield School, which was two miles from their homestead. Though Nellie was almost ten when she started school, she went on to become an outstanding student. She attended the Normal School in Winnipeg at sixteen, and was awarded her teaching certificate. That was her first step towards independence.

It was in Manitou, Manitoba, in 1892, that Nellie met the McClungs, who influenced her greatly. Mrs. McClung, her future mother-in-law, accompanied Nellie to political meetings and the equality between sons and daughters at the McClung home impressed Nellie deeply. She was not accustomed to male members of a household sharing tasks considered "womanly." In her own home, her mother Letitia had always made a clear distinction between men's work and women's, and Nellie used to be filled with dismay at the perceived injustice. She also befriended the oldest son, Wesley McClung, and he, shortly after, became her husband.

Meanwhile, her own political consciousness grew as she launched into the world outside the school room with another friend, a Mrs. Brown. She also joined the Women's Christian Temperance Union (W.C.T.U.) in Manitou, an organization which played an important role in her life. She knew that women worked just as hard as men but were not given the same privileges. To crown matters, many men drank away their wages and it was their wives who had to make do.

Once, she attended a political meeting with Mrs. Brown where the speaker was the Hon. Thomas Greenway, second premier of Manitoba. He claimed he was glad to see two women in the audience at the Town Hall. Nellie and Mrs. Brown had two questions for Mr. Greenway—was he in favour of allowing the women's vote, and when would women be given homesteading rights?

Nellie later reported her intense disappointment that Mr. Greenway chose not to address these questions at the meeting. He merely said that he knew politics concerned men as well as women, but that women did not need to be actually involved in the rough and tumble of politics.

"We were indignant at our chilly reception but undismayed and full of plans for further advances," Nellie wrote.

In the years that followed, Nellie married Wesley McClung and started her own family. She had five children, going on to write her first book, *Sowing Seeds in Danny*, published in 1908. It was a bestseller that year in Canada. Nellie's life was busy as an author, a wife and mother. She also continued to hone her public speaking skills. Her aim was to raise awareness about the status of women in the country.

In the text of one of her speeches, titled "Can a Woman Raise a Family and Have a Career?", Nellie wrote, "A woman can do other things while raising her family, and the family need not suffer, but she must have harmony at home. A woman can do many things if she has love and loyalty, and I have had these in abundant measure in my own home and in my own family…"

Nellie was conscious she was diving deep into the public sphere. When she became a mother, she became more aware of how crucial the role of women could be in public life. Her conviction that women could play a significant role in reducing the effects of drunkenness, hunger and poverty only got stronger as she plunged into Manitoba's suffrage movement.

At the Canadian Women's Press Club, she met with other like-minded women to discuss questions of rights and opportunities for women. At that time, noted British suffragette Emmeline Pankhurst visited Canada, creating a stir with her militant attitude. Nellie and her contemporaries at the Press Club decided that the immediate cause they should start working on was the plight of women workers in small factories. These women toiled in factories in cities like Toronto, Montreal and Winnipeg, routinely accepting long hours, low wages and no safety or privacy.

Along with Mrs. Claude Nash, Nellie decided something had to be done to bring the government's attention to this problem. They would press for the appointment of a female factory inspector who would at least understand the circumstances the women worked in. To achieve this end, they hit upon a novel idea—they would take the Premier of Manitoba, Sir Rodmond Roblin, on a visit to the factories, so he could see for himself.

Initially, Premier Roblin was hesitant to accompany the women. But they were just as determined to take him along and he gave in. On the way to the factory, he expounded on his views about women. He said he believed in the value of hard work for women and that they obviously needed "pin money," which they got through working at the factories. He also pointed out that perhaps Mrs. Nash and Nellie were being too sentimental about the factory women.

The two women kept silent as he went on. At the factory, they took him down "the dark and slippery stairs to an airless basement where light in the midday came from gaunt

light bulbs, hanging from smoky ceilings. The floor was lit-
tered with refuse of apple peelings and discarded clothing.
There was no ventilation and heat."

Nellie wanted him to speak to some of the women
there. But the premier was shocked at the place and clearly
uncomfortable. It seemed as if he was just waiting for an
opportunity to leave. Nellie and Mrs. Nash gave him no such
chance and shepherded him to a door marked "Toilet." The
premier was flabbergasted at the filth and lack of privacy.

After they left the place, the premier was stupefied as
to why such refined and well bred women as Nellie and Mrs.
Nash would want to associate themselves with such causes.
The premier however promised to look into the matter of
appointing a female factory inspector.

Nellie's dealings with the premier didn't end there. She
repeatedly asked for his cooperation in the matter of wom-
en's franchise. As a suffragist, she was sure that it was only
with the vote that women would have a say in the running of
their own lives. Nellie drew up a plan of action along with the
women at the Political Equality League.

On a Tuesday afternoon in January 1914, Nellie and
her colleagues went to the Legislative Assembly. They asked
for the vote. As expected, the premier rose to address the
assembly and, in rich fruity tones, described how that was
not at all a possibility. Nellie observed him closely, noting
his mannerisms, his speech patterns, his intonations. She

listened carefully to the words he used. He reiterated that the status of women was very good in Manitoba and indeed, in the Dominion of Canada, and there was no need for them to bother about the vote.

In Winnipeg's Walker Theatre the following night, a play had been announced. On stage was replicated the Legislative Assembly and the "legislators" were women. Male petitioners stepped up and began to make their petitions heard, much to the delight of the audience. They roared with laughter as the males requested items like banning of alkali on laundry soaps as it "ruined their delicate hands!"

The climax was, however, when a group of men arrived onstage and requested that men be allowed to vote. Nellie, as Premier Roblin, gave a scintillating performance, as she outlined the reasons why men should not have the vote. Gracious and patronising by turns, she imitated Roblin's manner perfectly.

"In this agricultural province, the man's place is the farm. Shall I call man away from the useful plow and harrow to talk loud on street corners about things that do not concern him? Politics unsettle men, and unsettled men means unsettled bills—broken furniture and broken vows—and divorce...when you ask for the vote you are asking me to break up peaceful happy homes—to wreck innocent lives."

The play was a resounding success and Nellie's performance clinched the deal. All of Winnipeg was talking about the clever burlesque. The mock parliament became part of the legend attached to Nellie and her fight for female suffrage.

The staging of the play was an important episode in the fight for women's rights in Manitoba. Using wit and sarcasm as weapons, Nellie and her fellow suffragists attempted to bring the issues they passionately believed in to the forefront. They succeeded, and the mock parliament introduced many people to the inevitability of female franchise. It was now only a matter of time.

However, all of these efforts on Nellie's part meant that her personal life was always under scrutiny. She was conscious that the public was always watching her. In those days, for a woman to be so visible in the public eye was something of a novelty. Not many women were brave enough to speak up in public. Many may have wanted to, but were held back by husbands, fathers and other family members.

It was quite common for a woman to find herself with no money or land and little education, dependent on the charity of her son or a male relative when her husband died. Sons got the property and unmarried women got no homesteading rights, despite possibly having worked on the family farm for years. These and other injustices rankled Nellie and she worked tirelessly to raise awareness about this social condition.

Her role as a mother was where she was the most

vulnerable. Rumours circulated that her children were suffering while their mother was out making speeches about women's rights. Thus she made it a point to begin her speeches with the words, "Settle down now, and don't worry about my children. They are well and happy and clothed and fed."

The biggest break for Nellie came when, along with a group of four other women, she became involved in the Persons case. It was the most significant piece of Canadian legislation for the women's movement. Under this law, which finally took effect only in 1929, women were finally recognized as persons, allowing them to be appointed to the federal senate. It was a revolutionary idea at the time. The process was lengthy, the fight bitter, but the Famous Five succeeded, laying down the foundation of the women's movement.

Nellie's contribution to the Canadian women's movement continued into her later years. She was the first woman to be appointed to the board of governors of the Canadian Broadcasting Corporation, on which she served for six years. Nellie was the only female delegate from the Methodist Church of Canada to the Methodist Ecumenical Conference in London, England, in 1921. In her speech there, she shocked the delegation by speaking about the necessity of allowing female ordination, one of her pet causes.

Nellie's life played out across the provinces of Canada. Born in Ontario, she lived and worked in Manitoba, British

Columbia and Alberta. Though politically she remained within the Liberal camp, she was, often, "not a good party woman." She worked across party lines when it came to women's rights issues.

By 1947, Nellie had slowed down. She still wrote articles and accepted speaking engagements from her home in Victoria, where she celebrated her golden wedding anniversary with husband Wes. Visitors did call, drawn by her wit and her stories. It was, however, increasingly difficult for her to keep up with the demands of her many admirers. Nellie McClung passed away in her beloved home, Lantern Lane, on September 1, 1951.

Chapter 9
Lea Roback

A garment factory in Montreal of the 1930s wasn't a pretty place. Indeed, very few similarities exist with any counterpart today. The grim buildings, with no separate washrooms for the sexes, though dark and ill-ventilated, provided a lifeline for poverty-stricken women. It allowed them to maintain a tenuous hold on life. These women, mainly French-Canadian and Jewish, endured the conditions at the factories because their livelihood and families depended on them. The women were herded like sheep to the narrow, dark benches, where they sewed desperately into the wee hours.

The finished products were worn by the elite of Montreal

and other big cities, most of whom knew nothing of the conditions which brought forth such exquisite workmanship.

Nor did they care.

In just such a factory in the city of Montreal, a fire broke out and the women struggled to escape their horrible fate. They rushed from their benches and beat at the doors, begging to be let out, while the fire climbed the windows and the air was rent with screams. Later, it became clear that many of the women would indeed have saved themselves if it weren't for the locked doors. Why were the doors locked? Management deemed it was necessary so that women who tried to escape would not steal the clothes they were sewing. It was a huge scandal, but for Lea Roback, it was not something she could swallow. Determined to undo this wrong, this fiery Jewish woman vowed she would never let such a preventable tragedy recur.

Lea Roback had a history of facing trouble head-on. She was born in 1903, a child of Polish Jews who had immigrated to Canada. The family lived in Beauport, a village near Quebec City, where her parents operated the general store. She shared household chores and duties at the store with her nine siblings. The house they lived in was small and hardly adequate for the large family. However, there was always enough to go around and the family was close-knit, intellectually alive and forward-looking.

Lea, the second of her parents' children, never kept quiet

Lea Roback

when she witnessed a wrong. For this she was often chastised. She recalled that her first experience with racism occurred when a customer in the store called her father names. Lea never forgot the sense of deep humiliation and righteous anger she felt. Yet, at the Roback home, subjects like these were always openly discussed.

The children spoke Russian, Polish, English, French and Yiddish. They were multi-lingual and curious, all of them interested in the world and their place in it. At home, the Jewish holy days were observed, though the children were not forced to take part. The siblings took the train to school, attending the Victoria School for Girls and the Quebec High School for Boys. Their mother was strongly opposed to sending them to a Catholic-based school. Lea took Hebrew lessons from a teacher who came to the home to teach, though this did not continue after Lea punched him in the face in the course of a disagreement. In Beauport, they generally had cordial relations with the townspeople. Her father's library was a talking point for many learned gentlemen in the town, who often discussed subjects like religion and philosophy with him. He was a co-founder of the Zionist movement in Montreal.

Lea's interest in social justice was evident from an early age. She took an active interest in the Jacques Plamondon trial that was agitating the whole of Quebec. The notes she made on the trial were kept in her family for many years. Jacques-Edouard Plamondon, a notary and public speaker, made an anti-Semitic speech in March 1910 that had unfortunate consequences in Quebec. There was a resurgence of anti-Semitic feeling reverberating around Europe and North America just then, spurred on by the trials of Alfred Dreyfus in France, Menahem Mendel Beilis in Russia, and Leo Frank in the United States. After the Plamondon speech, some Quebec youths had taken matters into their own hands and attacked Quebec Jews. This event polarized the Catholic and the liberal press, and various groups of the people. Plamondon was sued for libel. Lea followed the events by keeping a record of the trial.

When Lea was fifteen, the family moved to Montreal. Her mother was diagnosed with tuberculosis. It was 1918 and Lea searched desperately for work in Montreal. She did not have any intention of marrying and settling down, preferring to be financially independent. She eventually found work at Her Majesty's Theatre on Guy Street. She also worked as a cashier, a receptionist and in other similar positions.

In her later years, Lea recalled, "I was thrown out of two or three factories. But I always managed to get into a non-union shop. And we got the union in, in spite of everything. I was a real union old maid."

While working at these jobs she became aware of the deep-rooted differences between the ruling English-speaking elite in Montreal and the working-class Jewish and French-Canadian people. She was determined never to accept these differences. From that time on, Lea trained herself and learned to oppose inequality. She rose to become one of the country's foremost labour organizers and political activists.

While she was working, Lea saved enough money to study at university. It was her dream to go abroad and get a higher studies degree. In the 1920s, Lea left for the University of Grenoble in France to study literature, history and the arts. She supported herself by giving English lessons to students there.

In 1928, Lea's older brother Harry, who was studying medicine in Berlin, asked her to join him there. Being eager to see new places and to experience life anew, Lea left for Berlin and enrolled at the University of Berlin. Her subjects were Sociology and German.

Berlin at that time was not a place particularly conducive to learning. Compared to the coming future, it was quiet, but there were signs of the upheaval soon to follow. The Nazis were gathering strength—they had a paramilitary outfit but no representation in the government. The working class were disadvantaged by the disastrous ending of the First World War, and many of them had lost everything they owned. Thousands of Berliners were unemployed.

At the university, Lea was influenced by the flourishing left-wing student groups. She joined the Communist Party, finding in it an outlet for her passion for social justice. Lea learned the lessons of socialism, but the party was leaning more and more towards Leninism and Stalinism during those fateful years.

Slowly the Nazis grew more powerful. Anti-Semitism became more prominent. Raids by Hitler's troops became increasingly common.

She escaped detection several times because of her passport, which said "Canadian," and gave no indication that she was a Jew.

By 1932, Lea decided she had had enough of Europe. With troubled times imminent, she realized how difficult it would be for her if the fact of her being a Jew came to be known. She returned to Montreal that year, taking up a job at the Jewish Women's Y.W.H.A. She found a mentor in Saidye Bronfman, the philanthropist and community leader in Jewish Montreal.

However, Lea was not to be resident in Canada for long.

She joined a friend in Soviet Russia in 1934 in the middle of that country's revolution. She observed the atrocities and mayhem going on there and vowed to remain in Canada. By this time, Lea had also decided that married life was not for her. She would instead, devote her life to the fight against injustice. Once, when she was asked why she never married, in her inimitable style she answered, "I couldn't see myself ironing a man's shirt."

In the next year, Lea took over as manager for the Modern Bookshop, on Bleury Street. It was the first Marxist bookstore in the province and became a meeting place for left-wing radicals. Her days and evenings were spent in discussing theories regarding politics, women's rights and injustices perpetrated on the economically disadvantaged in society. She became acquainted with police harassment during this time. Lea always managed to connect with the common people, an affinity that was to remain till the end of her life, when she was still handing out pamphlets at the age of eighty on cold winter nights.

Meanwhile, Lea's organizing skills were being honed further as she coordinated Fred Rose's election campaign in the Cartier district in 1935. Rose, a Polish Jew who immigrated to Canada in 1916, was a Communist and union organizer with close ties to Dr. Norman Bethune. Much later, Rose would become the first Communist elected to Canada's House of Commons.

Dr. Norman Bethune, the surgeon, who strongly advocated socialized medicine, had a deep impact on Lea. She began to work with him, attempting to organize people who were jobless. Along with Dr. Bethune, she started agitating for better medical facilities to be made available to the working class. He believed that disease had not only physical and mental manifestations but, equally importantly, a socio-economic effect. Dr. Bethune was much concerned about how diseases affected the poorer sections of society. Lea, with her communist background, wholly agreed with Dr. Bethune's theories.

She realized how important it was for people to have access to proper nutrition. Her studies showed her that malnutrition was one of the major causes of ill health among the city's poor. Lea organized food donations from the elite of Montreal, while also promoting safe birth control as a means to limit large families.

In 1936 there was lots to do in Montreal, especially for a person of Lea's temperament. She met Thérèse Casgrain, a pioneer of women's suffrage work in Quebec. Both were on the same page and their attention became focused on the city's garment workers. Lea got involved with the International Ladies Garment Workers Union. Earlier, there had been little organized activity at the garment factories and it was only the committed leftists who had tried to instill unionism into the workplace. Attempts had been made to involve the French-Canadian and Jewish women who worked in the factories, but the Depression complicated matters. Most workers found it difficult to keep whatever jobs they had.

Montreal's garment factories employed many thousands of women, all of whom were ill-paid and worked in abysmal conditions for up to seventy hours a week. Also referred to as the rag trade, women who worked at these factories led a miserable existence.

Given the Depression, these workers had little say and were forced into tiny sweatshops, toiling non-stop in terrible conditions. The toilets were often just five feet away from where the women sat at their sewing machines. There were no windows. Worst of all, the foreman made sure that no one talked to her neighbour or even raised her head. The women were invariably threatened with dismissal if they protested. There were no holidays or vacations, and the women bore it all because they needed the money. Many were sexually harassed by the foremen, but quietly put up with that, too. As one former garment worker said in an interview with CBC radio, "We were treated like cockroaches, not human beings."

After the fire incident described above, Lea threw herself into organizing the ladies into a union. This gave them more bargaining power and a voice to oppose injustice. Their situation did improve, since now they had a collective voice. Lea was instrumental in organizing a twenty-five day strike featuring five thousand workers at the height of the

Depression in Montreal. The strike represented a victory both for women and for the labour movement. Conditions began to improve at the factories after that strike. No longer did the women feel that they were alone. They had realized the power of collective action, thanks to the organizing zeal of Lea and her colleagues.

Yet, in this too, Lea encountered opposition from men. The men workers said they would take care of the problem. She recalled in an interview that they said, "Leave it to us." "Thank you," she retorted, "but we don't like the arrangement."

Lea's next move was to organize, in 1941, a union at RCA Victor in Saint-Henri. The United Electrical Workers comprised the union, and Lea led the RCA workers into their first union contract. Half of the four thousand workers were women. Lea continued working with them till 1952.

Her conviction that unions were effective in securing fairer compensation never wavered throughout her career. Better working conditions and fairer pay was what she demanded on behalf of the working classes. The lessons she had learned from her parents—those of open mindedness and taking care of the disadvantaged—were reflected in her politics.

Throughout her life she represented workers in Montreal's factories, but she relinquished her membership in the Communist Party of Canada in the late 1950s. When asked why, she pointed out that she felt the things she thought important were not being tackled in the way she would have liked. However, her zeal for women's rights and issues of poverty did not diminish.

Lea patronized other causes and was involved with the Quebec Aid of the Partially Sighted. She was active within the anti-war and anti-nuclear movements, speaking with people, marching, leading demonstrations and handing out leaflets. Her struggles for equity in wages, access to housing, education and medical care continued throughout her life well into her eighties.

She was a prominent figure in the fight against racism and against the war in Vietnam. In the 60s, she co-founded the Voice of Women, a peace organization that rallied feminists all over the country. Lea was fiercely pro-choice and, in 1989, she participated in a rally supporting Chantal Daigle for the right to secure an abortion.

Madeleine Parent, Lea's colleague and fellow worker in the fight against injustice remembered her in an article written by Judy Rebick, "In her late eighties, I would accompany her on the bus because I was worried about her going home alone. She would insist that I sit separately so that she could talk to the person next to her. She would get them talking and then elevate whatever the problem or issue they were chatting about to a social or political issue. In that way, she raised the political consciousness of the people of Montreal, one by one." Madeleine Parent has credited Lea as being "a magnificent organizer."

That kind of grassroots thinking garnered her a great deal of support among the common people of Quebec. Her never-give-up attitude was evident in her talks with Nicole Lacelle, who wrote a book on her in 1988, "I do what I do because it is in my heart. If it succeeds, bravo: if it fails, I try again."

The Lea Roback Foundation was set up in her ninetieth year, as a way of commemorating her immense contribution to feminism and rights. The foundation awards scholarships to women from economically disadvantaged backgrounds who are interested in furthering their education. Lea died in August 2000 in an accident in Côte-des-Neiges at the age of ninety-six. Côte-des-Neiges is a neighbourhood, vibrant with immigrants of diverse ethnicities. That was Lea's residence of choice.

Chapter 10
Anna Leonowens

Though it was a sweltering day in August, the windows at the barracks were kept closed. This was to keep out the flies and mosquitoes that plagued the residents at the army barracks in Poona, India. Anna, then fifteen, waved her kerchief in a vain attempt to keep away those that did get in. Outside, in the sun, her brothers and sisters were playing tag. Raucous laughter at bawdy jokes came to her ears and she knew her stepfather loitered with his drunken mates just outside the door.

Anna's beloved books lay at the feet of her baby brother, who sat drooling on the floor, and her mother's tired sighs as she slaved over the stove caused her to shudder. She looked out the window. Far away, the mountain glimmered like a mirage in the heat and she wished passionately to escape.

Surely there was a life better than this, she thought. The Reverend Badger of the East India Company was always assuring her she was meant for better things. Her love of learning alone set her apart from the other army brats who lived in the barracks. Though it was seen as a chore even by her older sister Eliza, school to Anna represented a world where there was beauty, order and a chance at wonder. She had excelled at the army school and expressed to Rev. Badger her wish to further her education, or at least to postpone the inevitable fate that loomed before her. Marriage to an older man, a soldier from the barracks, most probably one of her stepfather's cronies, was unthinkable. There were so few opportunities for girls those days. Thus, Anna made up her mind. She would be accompanying the Reverend Badger on a trip to the Middle East as his scribe.

Her decision caused a great deal of talk in the barracks. Still, Anna was made of stern stuff and did exactly what she wanted. Then, once she returned, she got married to a young clerk in the British India service, Thomas Leonowens, to escape from the confines of her home.

After they were married, Anna and her young family moved all over the country in search of work. She was

Anna Leonowens

better-travelled than her husband and made all the decisions in the family. They had two children, then moved to Singapore where he was offered a job managing a small hotel.

Life for the Leonowens was starting to look up when disaster struck. Thomas passed away suddenly and Anna was left a widow with two young children, no prospects and no money. That was when the transformation began. From those circumstances, Anna Leonowens metamorphosed into a strong matriarch, an author, a woman's rights activist and traveller to distant lands.

It wasn't at all a simple process. Anna found herself teaching children in a school in Singapore. She was able to keep a roof over the heads of her children Avis and Louis, but a big break came her way when, by a stroke of luck, Anna was appointed governess to the King of Siam's children. Along with her children, Anna travelled to Siam (modern Thailand), and took up her duties as governess in the women's quarters. Though it was exciting, there were many goings-on in the palace that Anna deplored. Her interest in women's rights was born then as she saw the treatment meted out to the women of the harem. She did speak her mind at times and earned the king's respect but, for the most part, Anna grew more and more determined to send Avis away to Europe. She realized it was no easy task, bringing up a daughter in the atmosphere of an Eastern harem. It broke her heart, but Avis was sent to relatives in Scotland and she continued to teach in the court, living with her son Louis.

By 1867, Anna had decided to apply for a lengthy leave to see her daughter. Predictably, King Mongkut was not very keen, but Anna was desperate. She also made plans to enter Louis in a boarding school in Ireland. They left Siam, and Anna was never again able to visit that fabled land.

Her stay at the royal court, however, had given her many things. She had learned to be responsible for herself and her two children. She had become independent and capable of caring for her family without the help of a man. She was able to judge and to take decisions according to what her conscience and good sense dictated. Above all, Anna had developed a strong sense of kinship with women in the world and what they faced. It made her more sympathetic and ready to accept further responsibilities when she moved west, first to Europe to be reunited with her daughter, and then to North America.

Anna sailed to America with her daughter, Avis. The two of them opened a school, since that was the trade that Anna knew best. They had to struggle, but it was a peaceful life, away from the machinations and luxury at the royal court. Anna had deeply feared that the lax atmosphere at the court would have an adverse effect on her children. That was the reason she had sent Avis away. Her son Louis chafed against the disciplined lifestyle at boarding school in Europe, since he was so used to the easy-going court life in Siam.

Anna felt sure she had done the right thing in keeping Avis by her side and sending Louis off to boarding school. Her moving to America may have been influenced by her love of

Uncle Tom's Cabin, by Harriet Beecher Stowe. Certainly, she was filled with admiration for the strong anti-slavery movement in America, and she had often told her children and her students about the rousing nature of the book. Her blood boiled as she described the conditions slaves endured

In America, Anna visited a family named Cobb, and met many of their friends. At the Cobbs' request, she would regale her audience with tales of the Siamese court, and she was pleasantly surprised by the enthusiastic reception she received. Back at the school, Avis begged her put her stories into book form. That was the beginning of Anna's writing career.

Realizing that sustaining herself and Avis with the income generated by the school would be difficult, Anna decided to send some articles about her life in Siam to the *Atlantic Monthly*. The editor, James Freeman Clarke, liked what he read, and from then on Anna was a regular contributor. Buoyed by that success, she began working to put the articles into book form. Enjoying the recognition of her efforts in writing, she was on a fast track and suddenly in great demand as a speaker on the American lecture circuit.

Meanwhile, things were taking an interesting turn in her personal life. Thomas Fyshe, a young banker, had proposed to Avis and the young couple were planning a move to Canada after marriage. They wanted Anna to accompany them in setting up house in Halifax where Thomas was to be posted. Louis, too, had graduated from school and had moved to the Far East to find work. Anna knew that going with Avis and her husband would be a good move for her. Canada was a new frontier she was determined to conquer. She would also get to stay with her beloved daughter.

Finally, the Fyshes and Anna sailed for Halifax, where Thomas took up his new position at the Bank of Nova Scotia. Anna's reputation as a traveller and author had preceded her to Halifax, and she soon found herself in the midst of a set of interested people who flocked to meet and hear her.

Anna's energetic ways galvanized Halifax society. Soon she was caught up in establishing or joining numerous organizations—a weekly Shakespearean club, for example.

However, through all this talk of literature and high art, Anna noticed that there was also a very different side to Halifax, one that was seldom talked about in the drawing rooms of their set. She became aware of the poverty, disease and inequality of income that persisted in the poorer neighbourhoods of the city. Particularly drawn by the tales of lower-class women who struggled with disease and low incomes, drink and mistreatment at the hands of men and the system, Anna found it difficult to turn a blind eye.

She gathered together a number of women from her social gatherings who felt the same way and decided to do something for these unfortunates. Education and financial independence would be the only ways these women would be able to lead better, more fulfilling lives, Anna felt sure.

She compared the lives of the harem women from her days in Siam with those of the unfortunate women in Halifax and knew that she could put to use here the lessons she had learned abroad.

By the 1880s, women in Toronto had already begun to organize themselves and the privileged began to question what they could do for their less fortunate sisters. The women of Halifax, along with Anna, also began to make efforts to help those women who lived in servitude and degradation in the poorer sections of their city.

The next year saw a great change in Anna's life. She was offered the chance to tour Russia and write a series of articles about the common people, especially after the deposition of Czar Alexander II. Things were not very pleasant in that country after the Nihilists had taken power, and Anna's family were understandably wary of her taking up the assignment, which came from the American magazine *The Youth's Companion.* But to Anna, the idea was delightful. She was never one to turn down a chance at adventure. Her trip was arduous but exciting and she returned covered with glory. Once again she was in great demand as a speaker, and in many of her lectures her interest in women's rights came through clearly. She spoke about the hard life of Russian peasant women, and about the urban women who worked tirelessly to improve the conditions of the less fortunate ones, through education.

Meanwhile, in the prettily furnished Halifax drawing rooms, Anna continued her examination of women's lives in Halifax. One of her friends, Dr. Maria Angwin, had recently become the first female doctor in the city. She had horrific tales to tell about the lives of the men and women prisoners lodged at the infamous Rockhead Prison. Prisons were used not only for housing criminals but also for keeping people off the streets. Naturally they were filled to capacity and diseases flourished unchecked. Drink was a common enemy. Anna and her friends started working with the women in the prisons.

Around this time, the wife of the Governor-General of Canada, Lady Aberdeen, visited Halifax. Anna was one of the prominent Haligonians who received her. Lady Aberdeen was a woman who believed deeply in community work and she encouraged the city's Local Council of Women to work in conjunction with the National Council of Women in Canada, headquartered in Toronto. Anna was looking for just this kind of opportunity and jumped at the chance. She knew the city's poorer women now had a chance at a better life.

In 1896, through the Council, Anna was instrumental in passing a resolution to establish a school for truant children in Halifax. This was a cause dear to her heart, as she believed that education was imperative for a healthy life. Anna found out that children who were sentenced for truancy were sent either to St. Patrick's Home or to the Industrial School, both of which were actually reformatories for criminals. She argued that this only had the effect of hardening children to the criminal lifestyle.

She stated in the March 1896 report of the Second Annual Meeting of the Local Council of Women in Halifax in Association with the National Council of Women in Canada, "I think it is simply this...that no child who is simply a truant from school should be subjected to any influence but the highest, and that he could not possibly find in a mixed reformatory school."

Anna also took steps to increase representation of women on public school boards and other institutions. She raised the subject of the infamous Rockhead Prison and its inhabitants at city council meetings. Albemarle Street, too, was not the kind of place designed to inculcate healthy minds and bodies for young children. Anna convinced the council members that they had to take active measures to better the conditions of the children who lived there.

Anna realized that many of the women immigrants who came into Halifax were at the mercy of the male officers who often harassed them. They could be subjected to humiliation and degradation and, as they were new to the country, did not know where to complain. Anna moved a motion at the council that a female officer be appointed to deal specifically with the women who came into Canada. That motion was successfully carried.

Anna was president of the Halifax Women's Suffrage Association and was active in setting up the Victorian Order of Nurses, the National Home Reading Union and many arts organizations. The greatest test of her time came with the celebrations of Queen Victoria's Golden Jubilee in 1887. Anna was involved with many of the committees in the celebrations but she wanted something that would be a permanent part of the city's landscape. She decided to work towards the setting up of an art institute, which would offer vocational training in the mechanical arts like drafting.

Mainly through her efforts, the Victoria School of Art and Design was established in October 1887. The school exists to this day, a testament of the foresight of a visionary.

The main platforms that Anna fought on were the bettering of conditions for less fortunate children, conditions for better facilities for women inmates of the prison in Halifax, the introduction of a domestic science curriculum in schools and female officers for the new women immigrants.

Though her early life was a matter of debate and discussion among the socially prominent and well-heeled in Halifax, all that had happened long before she started to actually work for women. Once the Halifax elite realized her potential and her enormous courage, they welcomed her with open arms.

Anna did, however, leave Halifax and move to Montreal in 1899. Even there, though, she continued her work in advancing women's rights. Despite facing huge personal hardship when she lost her beloved daughter Avis, Anna continued looking after her grandchildren and remained a force to be reckoned with in both the Canadian cities she called home.

The veil she drew over her childhood and early youth slipped just a little, but now she is remembered with fondness in Canada for the changes she pioneered in women's lives here in the 1880s.

Chapter 11
Charlotte Whitton

An ordinary day in November 1962 turned out to be a momentous one for two key players in Ottawa's Board of Control. At the start, however, they had no inkling it would turn out quite the way it did. All they knew was that they were due to attend a city council meeting, and that there would be some sparring, some disagreements perhaps, but that city business would be conducted without any major problems. They were used to hectoring among their opposing camps, with a certain amount of rough words and heated debates. For Controller Paul Tardiff, it was a day he never forgot. For Charlotte Whitton, mayor of the city, the day's incident simply brought out all the latent frustrations she had been struggling with in her years as one of the few female officials in Ottawa.

The much-reported incident started with Mayor Whitton's relating how an official's civic duties could interfere with his or her family life. It was tough to balance both sides, she argued, in a startlingly prescient evaluation of the work environment, applicable even today. Everyone desired to have the best of both worlds, she said, giving equal representation to their personal and professional lives. As she was expounding on this theme, Paul Tardiff remarked disparagingly that, "she might have had children of her own if she hadn't been too busy with other things."

No self-respecting woman would take this. Charlotte saw red and, it was reported, "flayed wildly with her fists at Controller Paul Tardiff." "She swung at me four or five times but didn't get in a good solid blow," said the panting controller. "She was absolutely berserk." This incident, reported in *No Bleeding Heart: Charlotte Whitton, a Feminist on the Right,* by P. T. Rooke and R. L. Schnell, illustrates Whitton's image as a feminist with strong views about matrimony, women's rights and choice.

However, her sense of justice and fair play were strong. Some time later, in an address to the council, she mused on how the loss of Controller Tardiff from the council would be felt keenly. She said, "If, in truth, the mayor hopes now for a degree more of 'peace in our time' to the right of the Chair, this anticipation must, in no wise, be interpreted as detracting from full recognition of the lively mind, sharp energy, business acumen, and when he so chose, very real and valuable practical help and sound reasoning which Controller Tardiff brought to the dispatch of civic business."

In her lifetime, Charlotte faced a great deal of opposition from many quarters in her professional life. Vanquishing opponents was nothing new for Charlotte. In her career as a politician and social worker, she was a driving force in the fields of child and immigrant welfare. She crossed swords with misanthropic politicians and bureaucrats and refused to buckle to accepted notions of what a woman's place should be. In the Canada of the 1950s and 60s, her brand of feminism set teeth on edge, not only among establishment figures but also among other women.

But when Lottie, as she was known to her family and friends, was a child growing up in Renfrew, Ontario, there was little to mark her as out of the ordinary. In her adult years, she recollected with some humour her childhood passion for monarchy with its attendant pomp and splendour. In 1905, a royal contingent including the Duke and Duchess of Cornwall and York passed through Renfrew. Lottie was among the hundreds of supporters who lined up to wave Union Jacks. She was dressed in a stiffly starched party dress and box jacket, and absolutely thrilled to be witnessing royalty first hand. But then the little girl was sorely disappointed, because all she saw were ordinary-looking people with no jewels or outward trappings of elevated status at all!

Charlotte was born in 1896, in Renfrew, to John and Elizabeth Whitton. They were very much part of the Ottawa Valley logging community. Much of her childhood was blighted by her parents' holding opposing religious views, and early on she showed promise of an original mind when she refused to attend Catholic church. Her strong point was academics, and she revelled in performing well in school. She also had a strong bond with her paternal grandmother, who lived with them. Having been a teacher back in Yorkshire, her grandmother had a large supply of books, which Charlotte was encouraged to read. Early in life, she realized how being academically gifted could get her noticed, and she retained a scholarly outlook throughout her life, going on to accumulate accolades at school and university. She encouraged her siblings to pursue their studies so they could become financially independent, which she deemed imperative to a healthful existence.

School in those days wasn't at all a place of luxury. Students were expected to work hard in conditions that would be unthinkable today. Wood stoves heated the classrooms and students were expected to use washrooms located outside, even in inclement weather. Only those with a strong interest in education, or those with parental pressure, could persevere in these conditions. Charlotte thrived at school and, after she graduated from Renfrew Collegiate Institute, she enrolled for further training in subjects like Literature, Euclidean Geometry, French and Geography. Her six scholarships helped her secure a place at Queen's University in Kingston.

She ensured that her siblings also educated themselves so that they could go on to university. Her brothers and sister did go to university, just like her, which was quite an achievement for children from ordinary backgrounds with no special access to wealth or social contacts.

Charlotte enrolled at Queen's University, intending initially to become a teacher—one of the few careers available for women then. At Queen's, she was a pioneering spirit on the women's hockey team, and continued her studies for a Master's degree. Writing for and editing the *Queen's Journal* (in 1917, she became the paper's first female editor), corresponding with a large number of friends and acquaintances, and enjoying visits with her family characterized her formative years at Queen's.

Quite by chance, she entered the field of social work. While at Queen's, she came into contact with Dr. John Shearer, who had been involved with the Presbyterian Church's department of social service before being appointed to the Social Service Council of Canada. He was visiting Queen's with the express purpose of hiring young, promising graduates to work with him in Toronto. He founded *Social Welfare*, a magazine dedicated to the then-unregulated field of social service work in the country, in 1918, and was always on the lookout for promising students.

Charlotte, with her background in editing the *Queen's Journal* and her strong views and work ethic, caught his eye immediately and he hired her as his assistant editor and secretary. Her job was to manage the Toronto office and to liaise with welfare agencies in that city. He was a stickler for hard work, but taught Charlotte a great deal. She always had a soft spot for him, referring to him as "Mr. Greatheart."

During her time at the S.S.C.C. she came in contact with organizations like the Juvenile Court, the Neighbourhood Workers' Association, children's aid societies and settlement houses. She was involved with numerous bodies and, in the magazine, she produced a special series of articles on "Housing, Poverty and the Family" in September 1920.

Charlotte saw clearly that there was need to regulate the field of social work, to stop relying merely on volunteerism and to further its progress as a specialty like any other career field. Though she herself was untrained, she recognized the need for administrative guidelines and professional standards, which could only serve the practitioners well. Then the Depression hit in the 1930s, and governments struggled to accommodate the thousands of families who went on the dole. Charlotte argued that she could put into place a series of measures which would enable the agencies working in the field to determine just who the actual needy people were, and thus reduce the burden that was falling on R. B. Bennett's federal government. According to her, there were many who lived on the dole out of sheer laziness. She wrote a memo to the government entitled "The Distribution of Unemployment Relief," in which she urged that the government hire professional social workers. Thus she is credited with being a pioneering voice in the social work profession.

For her work in organizing social work into a profession, she was made a Commander of the British Empire in 1934, one of the many awards she was to receive in her lifetime. Also, while she was working at the S.S.C.C., she gained valuable expertise in the running of a charitable enterprise. She learned how to gather information, conduct surveys and then formulate the results into a workable plan. Her main thrust was social upliftment and, though some of her views on divorce and working women were controversial, it is evident that Charlotte believed in the emancipation of women.

As it was for many educated people in that time, eugenics was a hot-button issue for Charlotte. Concerned about how the country was shaping up, with immigrants coming in from all over the world, she had very strong opinions about who were desirable as prospective Canadians. In this, she agreed with many of the predominantly white, middle-class establishment figures in the country who were alarmed at the influx of immigrants who, they deemed, did not fit in. They had preset notions about the right type of person to be admitted into the fledgling country.

Charlotte's strong views did not extend only to Jews and non-English immigrants (neither of which she thought were desirable). She had a strong presence in the field of child welfare and reform. In the previous century, over eighty thousand children had been shipped from Britain to Canada. These "Home Children" often did have impoverished parents, who placed them with agencies so that they could lead better lives in Canada. But, naturally, this was not always how it worked out. The children often worked as cheap farm labour and, in fact, many had to escape to the United States. Charlotte was strongly opposed to the idea of importing children to Canada. She felt such children would weaken the future citizenry, due to their lack of a proper environment.

Charlotte's views on unmarried women and girls who gave birth would also grate on the nerves of later feminists. She had a habit of moralizing, and declared, in an article, that though the mother was to be sympathized with, she was in this situation perhaps through her own "stupidity." She considered that unwed mothers, particularly if they were domestics, must be of low intelligence and weak morals. These characteristics, she felt, would be passed on in the genes to their children, and would naturally contaminate the blood of Canada.

Charlotte Whitton

"The regulation and control of instinct and emotion as the basis of civilization, the training away from untrammelled play of natural impulses to a discriminate use and government of them is the whole principle of education," she wrote.

Another area which highlighted her feminism was nation-building. Her writing underlies her belief in the innate suitability of women for public office. She realized that it was to a large extent in the public sphere that women could hope to achieve some degree of "voice." In common with many feminists of the period, she was of the opinion that women should actively participate in governance:

"Only representation in the House of Commons and the Senate will afford women direct contact with national action. For this, the women of Canada must stand: for this they must strive, if they desire nay other office than that of 'Ladies Aid'...it therefore becomes the duty of every Canadian woman...to prepare herself for worthy citizenship. Never in any land has the need for intelligent womanhood been as great as in the Dominion of Canada today."

She also argued for equity in the workplace, convinced that discrimination on the basis of sex was a wrongful practice, since most women who went to work were doing so out of the desire to "earn their daily bread." She was, however, scornful of women who did not give their utmost to jobs, but leaned instead toward their families. She said, "...the part-time wife, part-time worker...doesn't take the nightshift ever; she doesn't take the weekend shift ever; she takes holidays with her husband and children when schools are on holiday, so will take little or no 'vacation' work shift."

Charlotte had little patience for understanding the many plates that must be juggled by women who work. Her narrowness in this respect is in sharp contrast to her views about claiming a place for women on the public stage. This contradiction has earned her a great deal of flak from historians and feminists. She agitated for equal pay for women in the workforce, but her writings about married women who work are unpalatable.

However, it must be remembered that there was a sea-change in the composition of society at the time. Many married women were being forced to work on account of the Depression, and there were fewer single women in the workforce. In the 1940s, a lot of argument was ongoing about the "right" of married women to work, their main argument being that they had mouths to feed. There was even one stream of popular thought that held married women were better workers than men, on account of their "greater sense of responsibility," as evidenced by a 1943 report entitled, "Post War Problems of Women." This was in direct contrast to Charlotte's views.

In 1950, there was a marked change in her career—she was elected to Ottawa's Board of Control. The next year she became mayor of Ottawa, being re-elected in 1952 and 1954. In municipal politics she earned a reputation of being no-nonsense and hard-headed. Her mayoral years continued in 1960 and 1962, after which she was defeated. She continued to serve as an alderman in Ottawa till her retirement in 1972. She passed away in January 1975, leaving an indelible mark on the national scene.

Later, criticism against Charlotte's legacy mounted, with allegations that she was anti-Semitic. In 2010, the Ottawa Famous Five Foundation recommended that Charlotte's name be added to the roster of "persons of national significance." Her contribution towards women's rights, politics and social work should be recognized, said her supporters. But her detractors, among the most vociferous being the Canadian Jewish Congress, completely disagreed. A Canadian Jewish Congress official was quoted in the *Vancouver Sun* on August 13, 2010:

"From our point of view, Charlotte Whitton is a troubling personality," said Bernie Farber, chief executive officer of the lobbying group. "On one hand, she certainly fought for the rights of women and fought very hard in that respect. On the other hand, there can be no doubt there were questionable activities she engaged in with relation to Jews.

"Certainly in the course of the Second World War and the Holocaust, she was instrumental in keeping Jewish orphans out of Canada because of her belief that Jews would not make good immigrants and were basically inferior."

However Charlotte's legacy is finally viewed, she is perhaps best remembered for one wry observation: "Whatever women do they must do twice as well as men to be thought half as good. Luckily, this is not difficult."

Acknowledgements

A book is never the product of a single mind. Many people have contributed to making this book happen. The project started with a desire to tell a story of women who were not quietly submissive, who dared to change the rules.

Professor Jan Noel, who I corresponded with at the University of Toronto, Mississauga, pointed out how there were many books on the second and third wave of feminists, but not many about the first pioneering feminists. I was, at once, intrigued. Thus the seeds were sown and I plunged headlong into a world very different from ours.

My thanks to all the librarians and archivists (may their tribe increase) at the institutions, whom I approached and who led me to the stories of "my women." This book is my attempt to imagine the world these women lived in, and the ways in which they effected change. Writing this book has been an immensely inspiring journey for me.

I would like to thank a number of people who were instrumental in my research: Susan Kooyman, Archivist at the Glenbow Archives, Alberta, for her invaluable help in locating documents; Lewis St. George Stubbs at the University of Manitoba, for pointing me in the right direction; Anne Lauzon at Ottawa City Archives; and Shannon

Acknowledgements

Hodge, archivist at the Jewish Public Library Archives.

A number of online sources proved to be very useful: these include the Manitoba Historical Society (www.mhs.mb.ca), the Historica Dominion Institute (www.histori.ca), Alberta Source (www.abheritage.ca), Collections Canada (www.collectionscanada.ca), the Canadian Encyclopedia (www.thecanadianencyclopedia.com), Famous Five (www.famousfive.ca), the University of Manitoba (www.umanitoba.ca), the Dictionary of Canadian Biography online (www.biographi.ca), the Government of Manitoba (www.gov.mb.ca).

I gathered material from Elections Canada's *Electoral Insight* magazine, from *Canadian Home Journal* and from the *Winnipeg Free Press*, though this list is by no means exhaustive.

On a personal note, I would like to thank Smita Misra at Queen's University, Doug Sherk in Ottawa, Dipayan Chaudhuri in Hamilton and Arundhati Chatterjee in Alberta for supporting me with this project. A special note to my daughters, Mimi and Ritika Chakrabarty—may you learn your life lessons from the stories of these women.

Sources and Further Reading

Bacchi, Carol Lee. *Liberation Deferred: The Ideas of the English-Canadian Suffragists, 1877–1918*. Toronto: University of Toronto Press, 1983.

Conrad, Margaret, and Alvin Finkel. *Nation and Society: Readings in Post-Confederation Canadian History, Volume 2*. Toronto: Pearson Education Canada, 2007.

Errington, Elizabeth Jane. *Wives and Mothers, School Mistresses and Scullery Maids: Working Women in Upper Canada, 1790–1840*. Montreal: McGill-Queen's University Press, 1995.

Fryer, Mary Beacock. *Emily Stowe: Doctor and Suffragist*. Toronto: Hannah Institute, 1990.

Gray, Charlotte. *Nellie McClung*. Toronto: Penguin, 2008.

———. *Mrs. King: The Life and Times of Isabel Mackenzie King*. Toronto: Penguin, 1998.

Hancock, Carol L. *No Small Legacy: Nellie McClung*. Kelowna: Wood Lake Books, 1986.

Prentice, Alison, et al. *Canadian Women: A History*. Toronto: Harcourt Brace, 1996.

Ray, Janet. *Emily Stowe*. Toronto: Fitzhenry & Whiteside, 2002.

Rooke, Patricia T., and Rodolph Leslie Schnell. *No Bleeding Heart: Charlotte Whitton, a Feminist on the Right*. Vancouver: University of British Columbia Press, 1987.

Sharpe, Robert, and Patricia McMahon. *The Persons Case: The Origins and Legacy of the Fight for Legal Personhood*. Toronto: University of Toronto Press, 2007.

Strong-Boag, Veronica, and Michelle Lynn Rosa, eds. *Nellie McClung, the Complete Autobiography:* Clearing in the West *and* The Stream Runs Fast. Toronto: Broadview Press, 2003.

Wine, Jeri D., and Janice L. Ristock. *Women and Social Change: Feminist Activism in Canada*. Toronto: James Lorimer, 1991.

About the Author

Moushumi Chakrabarty is the author of *Fighting for Women's Rights – The Extraordinary Adventures of Anna Leonowens*. A recipient of the Emerging Literary Artist Award from the Mississauga Arts Council, she lives with family and friends in Ontario, Canada.

Photo Credits

Index

Index